Harness the Email Writing Process

How to Become a More Effective and Efficient Email Writer

Paul Lima

www.paullima.com/books

Cover and interior design: Paul Lima

Published by Paul Lima, Toronto, Ontario, Canada www.paullima.com/books

Quantity discounts available for instructors and workshop leaders purchasing class sets. Contact Paul Lima – info@paullima.com.

Harness the Email Writing Process / Paul Lima.
ISBN 978-1-927710-13-5

Table of Contents

PREFACE V

CHAPTER 1: COMMUNICATION PROCESS...1

CHAPTER 2: PLEASED TO MEET YOU 3

CHAPTER 3: WRITING PROCESS..9

CHAPTER 4: CREATING OUTLINES 11

CHAPTER 5: WRITING EMAIL MESSAGES.. 17

CHAPTER 6: START WITH PURPOSE 27

CHAPTER 7: EMAIL SUBJECT LINES; HI/BYE; REPLY 39

CHAPTER 8: EMAIL ETIQUETTE..49

CHAPTER 9: CONSTRUCTING SENTENCES..53

CHAPTER 10: CREATING PARAGRAPHS 61

CHAPTER 11: TONING UP YOUR WRITING 67

CHAPTER 12: PROMOTIONAL EMAIL 73

APPENDIX ONE 79

APPENDIX TWO 85

APPENDIX THREE 91

APPENDIX FOUR...93

ABOUT THE AUTHOR 95

Preface

Welcome to *Harness the Email Writing Process*, a book written specifically for people who want to improve their email-writing skills and abilities.

This book is based on a business-writing course that I teach online for University of Toronto continuing education students and for corporate clients and private students. The course is based on *Harness the Business Writing Process*, a book that covers the writing process as well as writing email messages, letters, reports and proposals, web content and several other documents.

This book, *Harness the Email Writing Process*, is for you if you are looking to do any of the following:

- become a more effective email writer
- become a more efficient email writer
- make your points in a clear, concise, focused manner
- get your readers to take clearly defined actions
- get readers to take action by a specific date
- achieve your purpose when you write email messages

Harness the Email Writing Process will help you simplify your email communication by writing in a focused and concise manner. The book is all about communicating more effectively—conveying your purpose so your readers understand why you are writing and what action you need them to take.

When it comes to email writing, this book will get you grounded and focused—especially if you often feel as if you're spinning your wheels—by having you think before you write. You will think about your audience, your purpose and your desired outcome before you write. Then the book will help you effectively and efficiently write well-structured, focused email messages in a clear, concise manner.

You will be introduced to the business-writing process and come to understand the importance of following that process. Exercises in this book will help you apply the writing process to simple and complex email messages. In fact, I suggest that you apply the writing process to any writing that you do.

Make no mistake about it: writing is a process.

To improve your writing, you need to understand the process and apply it in a dedicated and disciplined manner. Sometimes you will strictly apply the process; sometimes you will apply it more loosely, depending on the importance and complexity of the email message you are writing. At all times, before you write, you must think about your topic, purpose and audience, and you need to get organized.

Following the writing process will make you a more effective, and ultimately a more efficient, writer. Effective means people will understand your email and take your desired action. Efficient means you will save time when writing your more effective messages.

Effectiveness and efficiency. When it comes to communicating, who could ask for anything more?

I hope you find the contents of this book both interesting and useful.

Note: This book should be 99.9% error-free. If you like to play "spot the typo," feel free to let me know if you find any errors or have any other comments about the book. Email info@paullima.com. (American spelling has been used in this book.)

Paul Lima
www.paullima.com

Chapter 1: Communication Process

Communication is a process. If you want to communicate effectively—in writing or when speaking—you should understand the process. Communication requires a sender who sends a message through a channel to a receiver. The process is not complete, however, without feedback; feedback closes the communication loop. Sometimes noise (competing messages, distractions, misunderstandings) interferes with your message; feedback lets you know if the receiver has received and understood your message.

When you communicate in person, you can ask for feedback—ask people if they understand what you are saying or if they have any questions. When you communicate in writing or through other one-way media (such as broadcast), it is more difficult to ask for feedback. To motivate and measure feedback, advertisers have learned how to use direct-response marketing techniques such as discount coupons, time-limited offers and so on.

Advertisers want feedback when they communicate so they can measure the effectiveness of their promotions. If they cannot gauge the effectiveness of promotional campaigns, how will they know whether they should run the same ads again, modify them or scrap them and come up with something new? If you do not close the communication loop in email writing, how will you know if the action you desire has been or will be taken?

Does closing the communication loop mean asking for replies from everybody you email? Not necessarily. In some instances, your writing purpose might not require you to close the communication loop. You might simply be sending information for the recipient to review—no action required. You might be making suggestions or recommendations that the recipient can act on or ignore. In other instances, however, you might have to know whether the recipient has taken action or has any questions. If so, you need to close the communication loop. Deciding whether to close it or not should be a conscious decision based on your particular business needs and your writing purpose.

For instance, if you don't care who shows up (or how many people show up) to a meeting, then there is no reason to ask people to reply. On the other hand, if you need to know how many people will be coming to the meeting so that you can prepare materials or arrange lunch, then you need to ask people to let you know if they will attend. Do you need a couple of days to give the caterer notice to arrange lunch? Then you need to ask people to reply several days in advance so you have time to notify the caterer.

The important point is this: if you need to know that the receiver has received and understood your message, then you have to put into place a method of closing the communication loop. If the loop does not close in a timely manner—timely as dictated by you and your circumstances—then you can troubleshoot the process. In other words, you can assume that your message has been received and understood and that appropriate action has been or will be taken, or you can build feedback into the communication process. With that in mind, as we work our way through this book, we will look at how to clearly communicate any required action and to request feedback in a timely manner.

It may seem odd to start a book on email writing with obtaining feedback. However, you communicate in writing for a reason that usually involves a required or optional action. If you do not spell out the action you want taken and close the communication loop, then you might not achieve your purpose. On the other hand, you might achieve your purpose and not know it because you have not closed the communication loop.

So where do we begin? How do we tackle this amorphous beast known as email writing? I suggest we begin at the beginning, with the business-writing process—a process that can be applied to any document that you have to write. However, our focus here will be on email writing.

Chapter 2: Pleased to Meet You

Just as there is a communication process, there is also a writing process. It's the approach you should take before you write, as you are writing and once you have completed writing a document.

If you follow the process, you will become a more effective writer. It's that simple.

You will also become a more efficient writer if you practice the process. However, as you read the first part of this book, you might find yourself thinking that if you have to follow the entire writing process every time you write an email message, it will take you forever to write one. Be patient. You will come to the five-question (W5) writing process shortcut for writing email messages, but I want you to understand the full process first. In addition, allow me to ask you this: Would you rather take a little longer to write an email that achieves what you want to achieve or take less time and not achieve your purpose? I presume you would rather do the former. If you do not achieve your purpose when you communicate, you will end up spending more time sorting out problems caused by miscommunication or ineffective communication.

Most people who follow the writing process find they become more effective writers and, as they practice the process, they also become more efficient writers. This point is worth reinforcing: it takes process-practice to become a more efficient writer; however, following the process will make you a more effective writer from the start. Being a more effective writer will save you time when it comes to sorting out business issues, and following the process will make you a more effective writer.

First introduction

Before you read about the writing process, I want you to take a moment and pretend you are introducing yourself to me. As you will see, I want you to write your introduction three times. To start, I simply want you to write the first introduction however you feel like writing it. Take some time now, before you read on, and write your introduction. I will explain how to write introductions two and three shortly.

Once you have written your first introduction, continue to read.

Writing process overview

Before you write your introduction a second and third time, allow me to introduce you to the writing process. The writing process includes five steps. Although all five steps involve writing, in terms of pen on paper or fingers on keyboard, only one step is writing as we view it in the conventional sense of the word—constructing sentences and paragraphs.

Here are the five steps that make up the writing process:

- Preparation
- Research
- Organization
- Writing
- Revision

Again, notice that writing is only one of the steps in the writing process. While we will examine each of these steps, for now I want to focus on why writing is a process and why, when writing, you should follow the five steps in order.

If you are like me, you fear the blank screen or blank page. You look at it and feel intimidated. You see it as an empty vessel you have to fill with words—only you are not sure which words to use, how to order them or how to use all the squiggles (known as punctuation marks) correctly. Perhaps you are not like me. Perhaps you love the blank page. You view it as a blank canvas, an opportunity to create. However, you may feel your creations take too long to come to fruition. You start, you stop, you start again. Moving forward is a slow, painful journey.

Writing seems to be painful in some way for almost everyone. For instance, when it comes to spelling and grammar, English is a convoluted and inconsistent language. For many of us, including me, spelling and grammar—let alone stringing words together in coherent sentences—can be frustrating.

You can improve your writing. All you have to do is harness the writing process, which we will discuss in detail.

Second introduction

I now want you to write your second introduction. This time, we are going to prepare using who, what, where, when and why—known as the W5. Before we look at how you would apply the W5, however, let's look at a few of the things you need to know before you begin to write almost any document:

- word count or page length
- due date
- audience and audience's expectations
- purpose or objective

We know this version of your introduction is due before you complete this chapter, since I am asking you to do it now. You can pretend you are going to send it to me to show me a sample of your writing and to introduce yourself to me. Since it is an introduction, not a report or a book, it should not be too long.

What do you think I, as your reader or audience, need from you? In other words, what are my expectations? Do I want your life history? Or do I simply want to know who you are and what you do in relation to why you purchased this book? Although the former might be an interesting read, will it be a practical read? The latter, on the other hand, is what you might expect me to want to know. Finally, what is your purpose in writing your introduction? Let's assume you want to tell me why you bought the book and what you hope to get out of it—how you hope it might help you.

Before you write your second introduction, answer the following questions in point form:

- *Who* are you?
- *What* do you do (or hope to do)?
- *Why* did you decide to buy this book?
- *When* did you decide to buy this book?
- *Where* did you buy this book?

Answer the above questions in point form. Then review your points and determine which ones you would want to use in your introduction. How do you determine that? Think of who I am and who you are, my (the reader's) expectations and your purpose for writing. Eliminate any points you don't need to make, put the remaining points in the order you should address them, write your second introduction and revise it as may be required.

Once you have written your second introduction, continue to read.

What did we do?

Consider the writing of your second introduction as an introduction to the writing process. How so? Let's look at what we just did:

1. Preparation
   a. defined the audience
   b. determined the expectations of the reader
   c. defined the writer's purpose
2. Research
   a. conducted internal research by answering the W5 questions

3. Organization
    a. organized the document into an outline (eliminated points you did not want to cover and prioritized the remaining points)
4. Writing (first draft)
5. Revision

The preparation, research and organization should have helped you focus on your reader, your purpose and the points you wanted to make. Therefore, you should have a more focused and concise document that helps you achieve your purpose. Shouldn't any business document be both focused and concise? Shouldn't it make sense to the reader and help the writer achieve a predefined purpose?

Third Introduction

So, are we done with our introductions? It depends. How long is your introduction? What "person" did you use? Did you use first person (I, me, my, we, us) or third person (he, she, they)? While business correspondence can be in first person, longer documents, such as proposals or reports, are often in third person. You could write a message like this: "Based on our second quarter sales, I have decided to give all of my employees a bonus." You are more likely, however, to write a message like this: "Based on second quarter sales, ABC Inc. has decided to give all employees a bonus."

Sometimes the choice of which person to use is subjective. For instance, I have used the third person in the "About" section of my website (www.paullima.com), where I promote my writing services and business-writing training. Here are a couple of excerpts from the page:

> A qualified adult educator, Paul develops and teaches business writing, email writing, report writing, advertising copywriting, media release writing and media interview training seminars for corporate and non-profit clients. He has conducted business writing, copywriting and business of freelance writing courses for adult education students at the University of Toronto, Humber College and George Brown College.

> An experienced freelance writer, Paul writes case studies, Web content, media releases, promotional brochures, ad copy and speeches for corporate and non-profit clients. He has written business profiles and articles on the business use of technology for numerous publications, including: *The Globe and Mail, National Post, Toronto Star, Backbone, Profit, Network World Canada* and other print and online publications.

Third person helps make the "about me" section feel credible; it does not feel like hard-sell content. Again, that may be a subjective interpretation. However, the distance of third person can lend objectivity and a greater degree of credibility to a document, as in this case:

> After reviewing the results of the recent product awareness survey, ABC Consulting recommends that 123 Ltd. broaden its marketing reach to include adults between the ages of 35 and 45.

By using "ABC Consulting" (third person), the document carries more weight. In other words, the company—not just one individual—is making, and therefore standing behind, this recommendation. Replace "ABC Consulting" with "I" and the statement loses power.

In addition, we often write bios in third person—perhaps to appear on a website or to be read by someone who introduces you before you make a presentation or give a speech. Third person also gives you a sense of distance from yourself. That sense of distance can help you revise your work to ensure it is as focused, complete and concise as it should be.

There are many times, though, when using first person is perfectly acceptable and even preferable. For now, however, I want you to review your second introduction. If it uses first person, I want you to write it one more time, in third person. Even if your bio is already in third person, make sure the length is appropriate for the occasion. Remember, you were asked to introduce yourself to the author of this book. Ask yourself what the author would want to know about you, the buyer of the book, and what you would want the author to know. If your bio is more than five sentences long, reduce it to no more than five sentences. In this way, you will more formally experience revision, the final step in the writing process.

Once you have written your third introduction, continue to read.
If you want to introduce yourself, email your introduction to info@paullima.com.

Pleased to Meet You

Chapter 3: Writing Process

There is a writing process short-cut for email messages; however, before we look at the short-cut, I'd like to take a more formal look at the writing process. As indicated, there are five steps in the writing process:

1. Preparation
2. Research
3. Organization
4. Writing
5. Revision

The time required to complete each step varies depending on the nature of the project. For instance, if you are a subject-matter expert, you might not have to spend any time on external research. If you write a particular type of document regularly, you might not have to spend much time on preparation; you might even have a template you fill in each time you write.

When writing a short email message you can prepare, research and organize by answering a few simple questions that I will soon outline. Answers to these questions will help you think about your audience and purpose, conduct internal research and generate the points (organization) you want to cover in your message. Once you have put your list of points in order (created an outline), writing should be as simple as turning the points into sentences and paragraphs. Then you revise your message to ensure you are making and supporting your primary point (conveying your purpose), proofread to check spelling and grammar, and hit send.

When writing a formal report, however, you will spend much more time preparing, researching and organizing. You might even have to produce a formal outline (an integral component of organization) for approval before you start to write. As you write, section by section, you might discover gaps in your knowledge and have to conduct more research and incorporate new material into your outline. When you complete your first draft, you will probably spend considerable time revising to ensure that your writing is as clear, concise and focused as it can be.

Writing process overview

Think of writing as a trip. If you plan your trip, you are less likely to get lost and more likely to arrive on time. That does not mean you cannot meander as you travel. You can. However, if you meander and your side trip takes you nowhere, you will find it easier to get back on track if you have a road map or, in the case of writing, a process that includes an outline. With that in mind, let's review each component of the five-step writing process.

As you read about the writing process, remember that I will provide you with a writing process shortcut for email messages. Before you get to the shortcut, however, you need to understand the full process.

Preparation

- establish your primary purpose (why you are writing)
- assess your readers (or audience) and their expectations and awareness of the issue(s) about which you are writing
- determine the detail into which you must go to achieve your purpose
- select the appropriate medium for delivering your words

Research

- determine if the research will be internal, external or both
- find appropriate sources of information
- take notes and document external sources

Organization

- prepare an outline, breaking down your document into logical and manageable chunks
- consider your layout, design and visuals (illustrations, graphs, charts)

Writing

- write from outline point to point, using each point like the opening line of a sentence; expand points into full sentences and paragraphs
- write with spell check and grammar check turned off
- complete a first draft, or a full section of longer documents, before revising
- write the introductions and conclusions of reports last

Revision

- revise with your reader, topic and purpose in mind
- revise to ensure the tone is appropriate for the reader and topic
- revise to ensure your writing is clear, concise and focused, and that it supports your purpose
- check spelling and grammar
- peer edit if possible

Chapter 4: Creating Outlines

Producing an outline before you write will help you write in a more effective and efficient manner. Again, if you are wondering why you have to go through all of this to write a simple email message, please stick with me. I am showing you the full, formal writing process now. I will soon show you a writing process shortcut that you can apply to most email messages.

Why create an outline?

Does creating an outline feel like work? Most people think it does. There is a valid reason for the feeling. It is work. On the other hand, what's the alternative? You can try to fill the blank page with sentences that will make sense to your audience and help you achieve your purpose. However, guess what happens when you try to do that? Your brain tries to write well—to write coherent, well-constructed sentences and paragraphs produced in a logical order—to spell correctly and to follow the rules of grammar. As it is trying to do all of that, it tries to keep track of what you have written, what you are writing and what you still need to write.

Now your brain is a remarkable organ. It can do all of that and more. What I am suggesting you do here, though, is relieve your brain of some of this workload by creating an outline—a formal list of all the points you need to cover placed in the order you feel you should write about them. An outline brings focus and logical order to your document. It lets you concentrate on writing each point in a clear, concise manner. Your brain won't have to remember what you have written while thinking about what you are writing and what you still have to write. If you follow the writing process, which lists editing as the final component, you can also free your brain from thinking about grammar and spelling as you complete your first draft.

With all this liberated brainpower available, you can focus on making your writing as effective as possible. After all, isn't that your primary goal—to write as effectively as possible?

Creating outlines

To create an outline, you simply jot down all the points you want to address—in logical order. Below are a couple of outline examples. The first is a major topic outline on the subject of creating outlines. The second is a more detailed outline on the same topic. The major topic outline includes the subject you are going to write about and, in this case, sets out the two major topics you are going to cover:

Creating outlines

1. How to create an outline
2. Benefits of outlining

To create a more detailed outline, you would add sub-points below the major topic headings, as in the following example:

Creating outlines

1. How to create an outline
   a. outline major topic points
   b. subdivide topic headings where appropriate
2. Benefits of outlining
   a. provides logical structure
   b. helps you detect errors in logic
   c. gives you a detailed road map
   d. lets you meander, if you wish, without getting lost
   e. removes the stress of trying to hold onto all you know about a topic while you are writing about it
   f. makes you a more confident writer
   g. ensures all major and minor points are covered, in logical order
   h. produces greater clarity and focus
   i. allows you to write quickly in manageable chunks
   j. ensures you do not lose your train of thought when you have to take breaks from writing
   k. facilitates the approval process, if approval is required
   l. lets you write from an approved outline
   m. *should* minimize revisions by superiors

Benefits of outlines expanded

Can your outlines be even more detailed? Absolutely. The greater the scope of the document (the longer and more complex the document), the longer and more detailed the outline should be. However, let me address some of the points listed under "Benefits of outlining" in the outline above.

Outlines provide a logical structure to your document. If you have brainstormed all the points you need to know and listed them in the order that you want to write about them, then you can detect errors in logic. I don't know about you, but I'd rather revise a series of outline points before I start to write than revise an entire document several times because my writing did not flow in a logical manner.

In addition, if you have a detailed road map to follow, it will get you from point A to point B in the shortest possible time. Instead of weaving all over the writing road and heading down dead ends, you'll start where you should start, take the route you need to take and end up where you want to be. (Notice how that last sentence was not in my "benefits" outline. However, notice how it is related to and logically follows the "gives you a detailed road map" point. That is the kind of focused writing that an outline can help you produce.)

A detailed outline means you do not have to hold on to all you know about a topic while you are writing about it. That removes a great deal of the stress that you might otherwise feel while you are writing and helps you write with greater confidence. If you are covering all the major and minor points you need to cover to convey your purpose or achieve your goal, then you will write with greater clarity and focus.

With an outline in place, you can write quickly in manageable chunks. Instead of having to write a fifteen-page report, you only have to write a series of chunks or sections. That reduces the stress associated with writing and ensures you do not lose your train of thought when you have to take breaks from writing longer documents. For instance, if the phone rings, you can finish a sentence, take the call and then pick up your writing at the next outline point. Or you can go home at the end of the day knowing you will come back to the document and pick up where you left off— because the next point you want to address is there in your outline.

If you have to get a major document approved before you can distribute it, send the outline out for approval first. The person who has to approve the document can see if you have covered in your outline all the points you need to make. If any points are missing, then she can add (or delete) points before sending the outline back to you. When you start to write, you will be writing to an approved outline.

That does not mean the person who has to approve the report won't make some changes; however, the changes are more likely to be of a subjective nature rather than a request to revamp and reorganize your entire document. I know, however, that some people who have to approve documents will ask you to revamp or reorganize anything you've written, even if you have carefully followed the approved outline. That's why I had points that said "*facilitates* the approval process" not "*guarantees* the approval" and "*should* minimize revisions by superiors" not "*will* minimize revisions…"

AIAA: attention, interest, attitude, action

Following the writing process, including the creation of an outline, will help you sell your readers on what you want them to do (the action you want them to take). If you are not writing a sales, promotional or marketing message, you may not think you are *selling* when you write. However, if you want your reader to take a specific action, you need to sell them. To do that, you need to do what advertisers do:

- **Attention**: capture the attention of your reader
- **Interest**: hold reader's interest by providing relevant background information
- **Attitude**: change or influence your reader's attitude
- **Action**: call for specific action

Depending on what you are writing, you AIAA, so to speak, by doing the following:

- Capture your reader's attention by using appropriate subject lines, titles and sub-titles, opening paragraphs and/or executive summaries.
- Hold your reader's interest with clear, concise, focused writing that reinforces their beliefs and expectations or enlightens them through the presentation of relevant information.
- Influence or change your reader's attitude by overcoming any objections they might have, informing them of the benefits of your position, stating your case in a logical and persuasive manner, supporting your arguments with relevant facts and/or by building trust in you, your position, your company and so on.
- Achieve your purpose by defining the action you want your reader to take, if action is required, and by asking your reader to take it by a specific date.

When reviewing your outlines before you write, ask yourself if addressing the points you want to make, in the order you have outlined them, will help you AIAA. If not, revise your points before you write. I don't know about you, but I'd rather revise a point-form outline than an entire document. And yes, sometimes your email messages will be simple and everything will fall into place simply by answering a few questions, as we shall see in the next chapter. However, remember that the more complex the message, the more important it is that you follow the detailed writing process, including the formal outline, if you want to be an effective writer.

Note on ASAP

By the way, if you believe calls to action are effective if you write that you need feedback or action ASAP, think again. I suggest you avoid using "ASAP" or even "as soon as possible" in email.

While ASAP means the same thing according to the dictionary to you and the reader, it does not mean the same thing according to the calendar to you and the reader. You might want an action completed by Wednesday afternoon, but if you use

ASAP the reader may look at his schedule and decide that Friday morning is as soon as he can complete it.

If you say something like, "Please return the report with your comments by noon on April 21" and you don't get the report by noon of that day, you can follow up by email or by phone. If you say, "Please return the report with your comments ASAP" you don't have a firm follow-up date. So if the date by when the action is taken is important, be as specific as possible in your call to action. Being specific about any deadlines related to achieving your purpose actually helps you help the reader help you.

Chapter 5: Writing Email Messages

Later in this book we will cover writing sentences, constructing paragraphs, using active and passive voice, writing in a concise manner, starting with purpose and conveying a clear call to action. You might want to read some of that before you read about writing email messages. However, from writing workshops I've conducted, I know those who primarily write short messages sometimes feel that following the writing process will add significantly to the time they spend writing email messages. With that in mind, I want to show you the W5 email-writing shortcut.

When you take the short-cut, you will still follow the writing process—that's crucial to becoming an effective writer. However, by answering the W5—who, what, where, when and why (and sometimes how or hoW, making it a W6)—you will shortcut the full and formal process.

W5 preparation, research and organization

When writing short documents, such as email messages, you can reduce the first three steps of the writing process—preparation, research and organization—to a few minutes using the W5 shortcut. You then write your message, edit it and click send.

If you are a parent, have you ever said to your child, "Think before you speak"? You know that if you think before you speak, there are some things you will say, some things you won't say and some things you will say differently. In short, thinking before you speak makes you a more effective speaker. Answering the W5 before you write an email message is you thinking before you write. It will make you a more effective writer.

W5 is the foundation of journalism. Answers to the W5 are used to outline the lead or opening paragraphs of any news article. Journalists, in fact, will tell you they do not start writing any article until they have answers to the W5 in place. There are times journalists find multiple W5 elements or need more than the basic W5 points before they write. There are times when they do not use all the W5 points they find. Either way, W5 is the place where they start. I am suggesting that W5 should be the foundation of all business writing as well—especially short email messages.

W5 news article outline

Let's see W5 in action. Review the following W5 news article outline:
- **Who**? Russians
- **What**? Held impromptu memorial services

- **Where**? At two subway stations in Moscow
- **When**? On Tuesday; brazen attacks a day earlier
- **Why**? suicide bombers conducted brazen attacks a day earlier that killed 39 people

From this W5 comes the article lead in *The New York Times*, March 30, 2010:

> Russians held impromptu memorial services on Tuesday at two subway stations in Moscow where suicide bombers conducted brazen attacks a day earlier that killed 39 people and stirred fears of a revival of terrorism here.

The full lead and expands a bit on the W5; the full article expands greatly on it and quotes various sources; however, once you have the W5, you have the foundation of the story. Sometimes, once you have the W5, you have the entire story. So the W5 can be the foundation of anything you write and, for short email messages, the W5 can be all you need.

Applying W5 to email

When it comes to writing email, answering the W5 questions can often replace much of the writing process. If you are writing a long or complex email message, I suggest you go through the entire writing process before you answer the W5 questions. For most email messages, however, answers to the W5 questions are all you need to focus on your topic, purpose and audience, as well as ascertain what you need by way of feedback, action or reply.

At minimum, answering the W5 questions (for consistency, I will call this the W5 even though there are, technically, six Ws when we include hoW) allows you to think about these points:

- Who: your audience and your relationship to the audience (reader)
- What: your topic or subject
- Why: your purpose
- What: details reader requires to understand your topic and purpose
- How: you got to the current state; you can solve or take advantage of the issue or opportunity
- What, when, where and how: any action, feedback or reply that should take place

Once you've answered the W5 questions, you can take these steps:

- review your answers and decide what you will include and what you will exclude when writing your message
- arrange points in the order in which you will address them—outline

- write from point to point
- revise as may be required
- hit send

In short, answering the W5 questions lets you prepare, conduct internal research and organize your thoughts before you write.

You can use the W5 to help you write any short message, which we will soon do. For instance, you can write a thank-you note, an apology, a complaint, an information request or any other request. You can use it to set up a meeting, invite someone to an event, request a project status update and so on. You can even use W5 to help write sales and marketing messages, although you will most likely cover additional points in your sales and marketing material, which is why it is important to think before you write and outline the points you want to make before you write.

What are readers looking for?

As you answer the W5, I suggest that you do it in a reader-centric manner. Think about what your readers are looking for and expecting. This would probably be the same thing you are looking for when you receive an email:

- subject line that captures attention
- purpose, clearly stated in the opening paragraph: what the message is about and why it is being written
- well-organized, clear, concise, focused writing that maintains interest (is related to your purpose)
- message length that is appropriate for the topic and purpose of the message; in email, most messages are one to five paragraphs in length
- closing paragraph that lets readers know if any action is required; if so, who takes it, by when, where and possibly how
- proper tone in relation to the message and your audience

With that in mind, let's go through the W5 process for several email messages and do some writing. There are some sample email messages in Appendix One; however, try the exercises below before you read the sample messages.

Thank-you note

I'd like you to think of someone to whom you owe a thank-you note or whom you would like to thank for a personal or business kindness. Before you do the exercise, make sure you have the name of the person in mind and that you know what that person did to earn your thanks.

Once you are ready, write point-form answers to the questions below on a sheet of paper or in a word processing file. I've included multiple W5 questions, most likely more than you'd ask if you were to do this on your own. However, I want to take you through the full writing process, including what to leave in and what to leave out (when organizing the points you want to make), before you write. To begin, answer the following questions:

- Whom do you want to thank? (Name the person and note that person's relationship to you.)
- Why do you want to thank him or her?
- What did that person do; what action did that person take?
- Where did it take place? When did it take place? How did it take place?
- What benefit did you derive from the action?
- What was your primary feeling or emotion?
- What overt action, if any, do you want the recipient to take? When and where should it take place? How should it take place?
- How should the recipient let you know she is taking action?
- What, if any, is your covert agenda (also known as your hidden agenda)?

Once you have answered the W5 questions, continue to read.

Before we move on, let's examine that last question. Remember all those thank-you notes that you sent to your grandparents when you were a child? You sent them after receiving birthday or other gifts from them. Although you were truly grateful, you probably resisted writing the note—until your parents told you that you might not receive more gifts unless you sent a thank-you note. So your hidden agenda was to receive more gifts. However, you didn't say that in your thank-you note, did you?

It happens in business too. Before you write anything, you should know what action you want to take place, if any, and if there are any deeper reasons for writing. You do not necessarily have to address those deeper reasons; however, you should be aware of them. That awareness will help you strike the right tone in your message. (More about tone later in the book.)

You probably think that you can write a simple thank-you note without answering the W5 questions first. You most likely can. This is just an exercise to take you through the W5 process. At the same time, I want you to know that your brain is going to try to answer the questions, with or without your active participation. It is ineffective, however, to have your brain thinking about answers to those questions as you are writing and editing. That is why we answer the questions before we write.

What you did when answering the W5

When you answered the above W5 questions, you went through the writing process. Specifically, here is what you did:

- established your primary purpose: why you were writing
- assessed audience: who they are, what they did, where/when they did it
- determined details you might include: how you felt, what benefit you derived, what action you want the reader to take
- conducted internal research: used memory as the source of information

After jotting down point-form notes in answer to the questions, you are almost organized. In fact, you probably have more information than you want to use in your final email message. Part of getting organized, however, is deciding what to include and what to exclude. Many writers will tell you that having more information than needed is a good place to be because it lets you think about what you need to say and don't need to say. This helps you focus your message.

If you are working on paper, highlight the points you want to address in your thank-you note. Once you have completed your highlighting, transfer your points to a word processing document. If you are working on your computer, copy and paste your research into a new file. Delete any points you don't have to express. (Save your original research in case you delete material that you later decide you need. This way, you will have it handy rather than having to recreate it.)

Decide where you are going to start, but keep in mind that readers want to know why (your purpose) you are writing. In other words, get to your purpose— "thank you"—in that first paragraph. Don't wait until the end of your message to achieve your purpose.

Once you jot down a purpose point, jot down all the other points you want to make in the order you feel you should make them. Remember, you get to decide what to leave in and what to leave out. With that, you have prepared an outline so that your writing will unfold in a focused, logical manner.

Write and then revise

Since this is a short thank-you note, you don't have to consider layout or design. You can simply write from outline point to outline point, expanding each point into sentences and paragraphs, as required. Write with spell check and grammar check turned off so that you can focus on writing your email message instead of editing it (the last part of the writing process) as you write.

When you have your outline ready, write your thank-you note.

Once you have written your thank-you note, continue to read.

Once you have completed the first draft of your thank-you note, review your work. Ensure that each paragraph contains no more than one significant point or ensure that the points contained in each paragraph are directly related. (See Chapter 10: Creating Paragraphs.)

Revise your draft keeping your reader, topic and purpose in mind. Ensure that the tone is appropriate to the subject and that your document is clear, concise and focused, and supports your purpose. Then check spelling and grammar.

Finally, add a subject line. Think of your subject line as an attention-grabbing headline. The subject line does not have to be in-your-face to grab attention. It should be tone-appropriate and allude to your purpose.

It is possible, even probable, that the entire process took longer than it would have taken you to just sit down and write the thank-you note off the top of your head. I hope, though, that the note you have written is as effective as, if not more effective than, the note you would have written had you just started with a blank screen. This process will help you write much more effective business email. In addition, the more you practice this process, the less time it will take to prepare, research and outline short messages before writing them.

You will spend less time writing if you are prepared, have completed your research and have a detailed outline in front of you. That makes you more efficient. The more prepared you are, the more complete your research is, the more detailed the outline is, the more effective your writing will be. The more effective (concise and focused) your writing is, the less time you will spend revising. But none of this will happen magically. It will only happen if you practice the five-step writing process—in the case of email, if you practice the W5 process.

As mentioned, there are some sample email messages, including thank-you notes, in Appendix One for you to review. However, I want you to try several more messages before you review them.

Apology note

Think of someone to whom you owe an apology—business or personal—and write that person an email message. Once you are ready, write point-form answers to the questions below on a sheet of paper or in a word processing file. I've included multiple W5 questions, most likely more than you'd ask if you were to do this on your own. Again, I want to take you through the full writing process, including what to leave in and what to leave out (when organizing the points you want to make), before you write. With that in mind, answer the questions:

- To whom are you writing? (Name the person and note that person's relationship to you.)
- Why are you writing?

- Why do you want to apologize to him or her?
- What did you do that you need to apologize for?
- Where did the action take place? When did it take place? How did it take place?
- What is your primary feeling or emotion?
- What is the recipient's primary feeling or emotion?
- What overt action, if any, do you want the reader to take? When and where should it take place? How should it take place?
- What, if any, is your hidden agenda?

Follow the process outlined in the thank-you note exercise and write your email. Before you write, review your "why." This is your purpose. Make sure you are alluding to your "why" in your subject line and state it in your opening paragraph. When you have written your apology note, review it and revise as may be required.

Once you have written your apology note, continue to read.

Complaint email

Let's complain or ask that a situation be resolved. You choose the topic:
- Did you have problems obtaining this book?
- Are you currently dealing with a problem with a superior, subordinate or peer at work?
- Are you having any work-related problems that are irking you?
- Have you had problems at a retail outlet or with a product or service?
- Are you having problems with City Hall or any other level of government?
- Are you having problems with a spouse, partner or child?
- Is there any other problem you would like to rectify?

Sometimes, when you want to complain or want a situation to be resolved, especially if you've been battling it for ages, you have to write a longer message. You also might find negative emotions or feelings creeping into your email. In this particular exercise, I want you to keep your message as appropriately short, succinct and positive (constructive or reasonable, you might say) as possible.

With that in mind, focus on the complaint or situation you want rectified and answer the following questions:
- To whom are you writing? What is your relationship?
- Why are you writing?

- What are you complaining about or what do you want rectified?
- Where, when and how did this take place?
- Why did this take place?
- What is your primary feeling or emotion?
- Why do you want a resolution?
- Did you previously complain to this person about this situation? If so, where and when? With what result?
- What action would it take to satisfy you?
- When, where and how should this be done?
- What action will you take if the situation is not resolved?

Follow the thank-you note process and write. Don't forget to delete any points you don't need to include in your message once you create your initial outline. The goal is to have on paper only the points you want to address, in the order you should address them. Also, ensure your purpose is clear and up front. Revise as may be required and you are done.

Once you have written your complaint note, continue to read.

Final email exercise

Before you look at the sample email messages in Appendix One, complete one more email-writing exercise. For this final exercise, I'd like you to write a business or work-related email message. Feel free to come up with your own idea for this email message; however, if you need an idea, here are some suggestions you can choose from:

- arrange a meeting
- query a tardy supplier
- request an overdue payment
- report on progress to a colleague, supplier or vendor
- move back a project deadline
- request assistance on a project
- request required information

Before you write, come up with the W5 questions you want to answer to help you think about your reader, conduct internal research and organize your thoughts.

Answering the W5 first will help you prepare, research and outline your email. Outlining your email will help you focus your writing. If your writing is focused (follows a thoughtful outline), you should spend less time revising. You will still revise, but you will be revising a solid first draft.

If you feel you need a bit of help writing sentences and paragraphs, look at Chapters 9 and 10 (Constructing Sentences and Creating Paragraphs).

Once you have written your work-related note, continue to read.
Again, see sample emails in Appendix One toward the end of this book.

Chapter 6: Start with Purpose

As a freelance writer and business-writing trainer, I have to send the occasional bill collection message to clients. When I send an email message, approximately forty-five days after sending an invoice that was due in thirty days, what do you think my purpose is?

"To get paid" is correct because I want to be paid. However, I also want to maintain my relationship with the client. If my tone is negative, accusatory and unprofessional, I might receive my payment; however, I would probably lose the client. If my first message accuses the client of willful nonpayment and if I threaten to send in a collection agency or to take the client to small claims court, the client might pay me, but why would the client want to work with me again?

In short, what you want to do is start any email with your purpose, but you also want to make sure the overall tone of your message is appropriate to the situation. Working your purpose into the opening of any document—from a simple email message to a major report—ensures that the reader reads all that follows with your purpose in mind.

On occasion, people tell me that starting with purpose feels too abrupt or impolite. My reply? Starting with purpose is effective. For instance, the message below may seem polite, but is it effective?

> How are you? Hope all is well and that you are not too busy. Hey, maybe we can do lunch next week? I need your feedback on the environmental report ASAP so I can submit it...

If you start with your purpose, you are more inclined to write:

> We need to submit the attached environmental report to the ministry by the end of the month so we can obtain funding. Your feedback is required by April 21 before the report can be submitted.

As the reader of the message, I know why you are writing (to get my feedback on the attached report), what I have to do, why I have to do it (the benefits of doing it) and when I have to do it by. How effective is that?

Purpose eliminates mystery

When you are writing formal business documents, you are not writing mystery novels. The reader should not have to unravel your purpose. Instead, you should lead with your purpose. For instance, say you want to inquire about leasing cars for your company from an automotive company. Presumably, your purpose would be to receive a quote from the company. With that in mind, organize the following sentences in the order you would address them, starting with purpose:

1. General Engines has an excellent reputation for reliable service.
2. We're looking for the best lease price, coupled with reliable service.
3. We would like to receive a quote on the lease of four XK4s.
4. Call us by October 30 to discuss our needs, before issuing the quote.
5. We would like to do business with the local dealer.

Place the points in the order, starting with your purpose, before you read on.

Imagine if you had the above five points in front of you before you started to write. What you would do next is:

- decide which of the points you should address
- decide which, if any, you should not address
- organize the points you want to address in terms of where you should start, what you should write next and so on

At that point, it's all over but the writing. Write from point to point and you are done. That is the power of organization, no matter what type of document you are writing. Being able to jot down the points you need to address (creating your outline) comes from knowing what you need to say to accomplish your purpose.

With that in mind, here is my suggested order, starting with purpose:

1. We would like to receive a quote on the lease of four XK4s.
2. We're looking for the best lease price, coupled with reliable service.
3. General Engines has an excellent reputation for reliable service.
4. We would like to do business with the local dealer.
5. Call us by October 30 to discuss our needs, before issuing a quote.

If I am the leasing manager and I receive this inquiry, I will start thinking about how I can help you—how I can meet your purpose—based on the first point. But what if the leasing manager has moved to the parts department and you don't know it? If I am the former leasing manager, I will open your email message and, based on your first point, I will redirect your email to the appropriate person at the dealership. Again, by starting with purpose, you help the reader help you. Not only is your purpose more likely to be met, you are saving the reader time. He does not have to spend time wondering what your email is about.

Once you have your points in order, you write. For example, you might convert your points into a letter like this:

Dear Mr. Lease Manager:

ABC Inc. is looking to receive a quote on the lease of four XK4s. We are interested in the best lease price, coupled with reliable service, <u>for which General Engines has an excellent reputation</u>.

We would like to receive a quote from your local dealer. Please call us by October 30 to discuss our needs in detail, before issuing the quote.

Depending on your relationship with the company, you might want to give the dealership some background information about your organization. If so, the points that you want to address should be in your outline before you start to write. If you are putting out a formal tender, you might want to direct the reader to an attachment. No matter what, though, you want to state your purpose. That way, your reader will be reading your message with your purpose in mind.

Notice in the above letter that that I have underlined this phrase "for which General Engines has an excellent reputation." I call such phrases window dressing. They may be nice to write but they do not advance your cause. So why use them? There is no reason to do so. If you cut the phrase, would it be missed? If not, cut it.

Am I adamantly opposed to window dressing? Let me answer the question with a question: How does it help you? If you have one window-dressing phrase in a letter or an email message, it most likely will not interfere with your communication. If you have one or two window-dressing phrases every paragraph or two, however, your document will not be as clear, concise or coherent as it could be, and should be. That will interfere with the effectiveness of your communication.

Purpose exercise

Let's do another exercise. Your purpose is to have the recipient of your message send you a copy of a presentation delivered at the NACB convention to use within your organization. Pick the sentence that *best states your purpose*. You don't have to put the sentences in order; just pick the one that best states your purpose.

1. I heard good things about the speech you presented at NACB.
2. Several managers in my firm have asked me to write you regarding your speech at NACB.
3. Our consulting firm would like to obtain a copy of the speech you gave at NACB last week so we can circulate it internally.
4. As you may know, our company deals with some of the issues you raised recently in your speech at the NACB convention.
5. Do you lend or sell your speeches?

Pick the sentence that best states your purpose, before reading on.

When I conduct workshops based on this book, 95% of the participants pick the third sentence as the one that best states the purpose, and I agree with them. Many participants also say that they would not start their letter with that statement, and I don't have a problem with that.

As I have been saying, you should start with purpose. However, you do not have to state your purpose in your opening sentence. You need to define your purpose clearly so you can convey it clearly. However, you also have to determine if your purpose sentence will be your opening sentence, middle sentence or the final sentence of your opening paragraph. In other words, you have some latitude—as long as you work your purpose (consider it your topic sentence; see Chapter 9 on Writing Sentences) into your opening paragraph.

With that in mind, your opening paragraph could read something like this:

> **I heard good things from my staff about the speech you presented at the NACB convention. As you may know, our company deals with some of the issues you raised in your speech. We would like to obtain a copy of the speech you gave at the conference so we can circulate it internally. We are willing to discuss any fee that may be associated with this.**

Notice that our purpose is the second last sentence. The reader does not personally know the writer, so there is nothing wrong with providing a bit of background information before hitting the purpose statement.

The writer knows that some people who give presentations often give them or sell them to companies, so right after he conveys his purpose the writer overcomes any objection the reader might have by ensuring that the reader knows the writer is willing to pay for the speech. The writer has captured attention, held interest, influenced attitude—all in one paragraph. And the writer has all but asked for action.

If the reader gives away copies of speeches, he can say so. If the reader sells copies of speeches, he can let the writer know what the cost will be. At the same time, if the writer is not willing to pay for a copy of the speech, the writer should not use the last sentence. The point is this: Do you see how much you can pack into a paragraph when you think about what you want to say and write in a clear, concise and coherent manner? Such writing stems from knowing your purpose and organizing your thoughts (creating an outline) before you write.

Exceptions?

I once gave a workshop based on this book to a group of teachers who resisted my "start with purpose" message. When they returned from summer vacation, they had a lot of business information to communicate with each other, yet they felt it was rude not to ask other teachers how their holidays were when communicating for the first time after coming back from holidays. I made three suggestions:

- Send a "how are you, how were your holidays" email separate from any business email messages to get the informal message out of your system.
- Open your first business message with a one-line paragraph: "Welcome back. Hope you enjoyed your holidays." Make sure your purpose is clearly stated in the next paragraph. The paragraph separation helps the reader separate the short personal message from the business message.
- Open with purpose. Write the body of your message, including action statement. Include a short personal message as a separate paragraph at the end of your message. Perhaps something like this: "I look forward to hearing about your holidays when we meet in the staff room."

I am not asking you to be unfriendly or rude. I am asking you to be effective and efficient. If you are clear, you are more likely to be understood and achieve your objective. So stay focused on the business issue. If it helps, ask yourself this question before you write: What is the consequence of being misunderstood and not accomplishing my objective?

If there are absolutely no consequences, you might ask yourself if you even need to send the message. If there are minor or major consequences, you will—I presume—want to be as clear as possible and not muddy your business writing with personal statements.

Soft entry

The teachers had another issue, one that I can imagine anyone in customer service having or, frankly, anyone who has to write about a delicate subject.

The teachers wanted what they described as a "soft entry" into writing difficult email messages, messages about negative issues that had to be sent to the parents of students. I stressed the need to clearly define purpose and allude to it in the subject line so they could capture the attention of the parents. In other words, even if a message is negative, you do not want to keep your reader in suspense. However, that does not mean you slap your reader across the face.

The need for a "soft entry" comes from the fact that defining purpose can be difficult, whether you are a teacher or in business. For instance, a teacher described the following scenario:

> What if a good student goes bad? One day he gets into an argument with another student. Another day he falls asleep in class. These would be dealt with by the teacher; the parents would not need to be notified. Then the student sets off firecrackers at the back of the class. This is something for

which he could be suspended and, of course, the parents would have to be notified. Do I start my email with "Dear Parents: Your son set off firecrackers in class today and may be suspended"?

My answer: Define your *true* purpose. To help you do that, ask yourself what the parents know, don't know and need to know. For instance, based on previous reports, the parents know their son is well behaved and gets good marks. The parents don't know about the behavioral shift. They need to know about it and about your concerns. Therefore, the purpose is not to notify the parents that the student could be suspended. The purpose is to notify the parents of the shift in behavior and your concern. As the teacher, you want to set up a meeting to discuss the situation, but that is not your purpose. Setting up a meeting is the action that you want to take place. Don't confuse your purpose with your action. Both are important but you want to know which is which.

Watch how we can have a so-called soft entry that states our true purpose as we have defined it. In other words, there is no need to start with "how are you and how are things?" (which would be silly under the circumstances). Nor is there a need to start with the possibility of a suspension.

Below is the email we developed. Notice how we allude to our purpose in the subject line and make it clear in our opening paragraph. In short, by the end of the first paragraph, we have achieved our purpose, which is to express concern over the student's shift in behavior. By the end of the email, we have asked for action based on our purpose. In between, we let the parents know that suspension is an option (not that it will happen), so we have even spelled out the consequences that could occur (not an overt threat) if there is no return to proper deportment.

Subject: Shift in Tommy's behavior at school

Dear Mr. and Mrs. Smith,

As you know, Tommy has been an excellent student who gets great marks. Recently, his behavior has started to change and we are concerned. Last week, he initiated an argument with another student and he fell asleep in class. Yesterday, he set off firecrackers at the back of the class.

We did not notify you of the first two incidents because they were minor and Tommy promised to settle down. However, the firecracker incident is serious. Students can be suspended for engaging in such behavior.

Before we take any action whatsoever, we would like to meet with you to discuss the situation. Can you please notify me in the next day or two when you will be able to meet after school? I look forward to your phone call or email.

Notice that by clearly defining your true purpose you can allude to it in the subject line and state it in the first paragraph. In addition, we have a soft but appropriate opening. Following your purpose—expressing your concern over the shift in Tommy's behavior—you give the parents appropriate background information that keeps them interested and influences their attitude. Then you state your call to action.

A couple of teachers said they would prefer to phone the parents rather than send an email. In this case, I'd encourage it. However, before making such a call you would still want to organize your thoughts and compose the message you want to convey. If you called, you would identify yourself and ask if the parent had a moment to talk. Then you would essentially deliver the message above and let the parent respond. In other words, you would still convey your purpose, your reason for calling, up front.

Practice putting purpose first

Read the following short case studies below. When you finish reading each case study, jot down your purpose and the action you would like the reader to take. Ask yourself: What is my true business purpose? What do I want to achieve? Why? What action would I like to see the reader take?

Case Study One: Hotel

On business trips to London, Ontario, you stay at the Chelsea Hotel. On your most recent trip, conditions were below expected standards. The room was not clean and dining room service was poor. In addition, the rates had been increased 5%. You travel to London every quarter on business. Your company has used this hotel for several years because it is conveniently located and, even with the recent price increase, offers reasonable rates.

◼ ◼ ◼

Case Study Two: Furniture

On November 1, you ordered furniture from the Office Company catalogue. Your order arrived on November 7, but two chairs were missing. You called and spoke to Harry who said he would take care of it. On November 11, one chair arrived; it was the wrong color. You called and found out that Harry had quit. Nobody else knew about your problem. The person you talked to asked you to email details to the manager.

Once you have written down your purpose, and the action you would like to see each reader take, compose opening paragraphs for each of the case studies. (You can review sample openings for each case study in Appendix Two.)

Determine your business purpose for each case study and write an opening paragraph. Do this before you read the opening paragraphs in Appendix Two.

From purpose to conclusion

Of course, when you write email you have to do more than start with purpose. You have to write from purpose to conclusion. That is where creating a detailed outline comes into play. Creating your outline—all the points you want to make, in the order you should make them—will enable you to write from purpose to conclusion, as in the example below.

> **Subject**: Meeting to discuss pricing concerns
>
> Hi Chris,
>
> I would like to meet to discuss some concerns over the recent proposal to increase the price of widgets you supply to Acme Manufacturing.
>
> Retailers such as Floor-Mart are exerting pressure on margins and I would like to reach a pricing arrangement with you before we place our fourth quarter order in August.
>
> I am available to meet the week of June 18 to discuss your proposal. I will call you on Wednesday to set up a date, time and location for the meeting. If you have any questions, please email or call me.

The purpose is to meet about a specific issue, so it is no surprise that we see the word "meeting" in the subject line and we see the word "meet" in the opening paragraph. But we also see the reason for the meeting—pricing concerns—and why the writer is concerned (Floor-Mart is exerting pressure on margins). That is an attitude-adjusting concern that will get the reader thinking about agreeing to meet. In other words, while the ultimate purpose is to get a price reduction, the purpose of this email is to set up a meeting to talk about it. The fact is one would most likely not achieve the desired price reduction without meeting, so the writer knows he has to set up the meeting (purpose) first. With that in mind, let's continue to practice defining your true business purpose and putting your purpose first. In addition, let's write from purpose to conclusion or request for action.

Continue purpose practice

The next two exercises have you writing email messages that address more complex negative situations. At first blush, it might look like you have to write a collection email for one of the case studies below and a complaint email for the other. However, there is a catch. The case studies give you insight into both sides of the same issue. The hope is that by seeing that there are at least two sides to this issue (there are always at least two sides to issues) you will be able to write concise, coherent, focused email messages that state your case in a professional, positive and logical manner. You might even see that your purpose is not to write collection and complaint letters. But I will leave that decision up to you.

To begin the exercise, read the two case studies below before you write.

Case Study A: Trinket Ltd.'s issue

Widgets are a main component used in the manufacturing of your product, Trinkets. For the last year, you have been ordering widgets in bulk—25,000 units per month—from Widget Inc.

Widget ships you 25,250 units on a just-in-time basis but only charges you for 25,000 because there is an agreed upon possible fault level of up to 1%. (This arrangement is common in manufacturing.)

Widget Inc.'s prices are competitive. You pay 50% down ($10,000) and the balance two weeks after delivery. If your payment is late, as it has been three times in the past year due to the installation of a new accounting system, you are charged a 2% late fee on the next invoice. However, Widget waived the penalty fee twice.

You have had a solid business relationship with Widget Inc. (You are not friends with your counterpart. You met him twice—once for lunch when negotiating the deal and once at a Chamber of Commerce meeting.)

In the first four months, two of Widget's shipments were several hours late, causing you minor production delays but the delivery issues have been resolved. However, your last shipment was short (24,950 widgets were shipped) and the fault level was high (1.5%), leaving you with 24,575 widgets.

Although you had surplus widgets from previous shipments, you were not able to cover all your orders, which were higher than expected. In the end, you short-shipped Trinkets to your major client, Floor-Mart. Floor-Mart sent you an angry email, threatening to find another supplier, and invoked a penalty clause in your contract, which cost you 5% ($5,000) on a $100,000 invoice.

You have decided to withhold the final payment on the last batch of widgets until you have resolved the issue. You are now going to write an email to your counterpart at Widget Inc.

You are the CEO of Trinket Ltd., the top cheese, not an accounting manager or clerk. Write an email to the CEO of Widget Inc.

Note: Before you write, determine your business purpose and the action you want to see the reader take. Write a business email, using an appropriate tone, meant to achieve your purpose. Include your purpose in your subject line and opening paragraph.

◨ ◨ ◨

Case Study B: Widget Inc.'s issue

Widgets are an important component used in the manufacturing of Trinkets. For the last year, Trinket Ltd. has been ordering widgets in bulk—25,000 units per month—from your company.

You ship 25,250 units on a just-in-time basis but only charge for 25,000 as there is a fault level of up to 1%. Trinket understands and accepts this fault level.

Your products are competitively priced. Trinket Ltd. pays 50% down ($10,000) and the balance two weeks after delivery. If payment is late, as it has been three times, you charge a 2% fee on the next invoice. However, as a gesture of good will, you waived the late fee the first two times payments were late.

You have had a solid business relationship with your counterpart at Trinket. (You are not friends with your counterpart. You met him twice—once for lunch when negotiating the deal and once at a Chamber of Commerce meeting.)

Early on, you shipped two orders several hours late, causing Trinket minor production delays. You thought you had resolved delivery issues; however, your last shipment of widgets was short (24,950 widgets were shipped) and the fault level was high (1.5%), due to machine repair problems caused by a third-party maintenance company. You were not concerned because you believed Trinket had surplus widgets from previous shipments and could cover its orders.

Your accounts receivable clerk received a call from the Trinket accounts payable clerk explaining that Trinket was unable to cover all its orders. Trinket's major client, Floor-Mart, is threatening to find another supplier and has invoked a penalty clause, which cost Trinket $5,000.

Trinket's payment is overdue. You are now going to write an email to your counterpart at Trinket.

You are the CEO of Widget Inc., the top cheese, not an accounting manager or clerk. Write a letter to the CEO of Trinket Ltd.

Note: Before you write, determine your business purpose and the action you want to see the reader take. Write a business email, using an appropriate tone, meant to achieve your purpose. Include your purpose in your opening paragraph.

I recommend that you do your preparation work and outline the points you will address in your email messages, in the order in which you will address them. To help you organize your thoughts, answer the following W5 questions:

- Why are you writing? (What is your business purpose?)
- Who did what to whom, when and where?
- What was the consequence?
- Why did this happen?
- What action do you want to see take place?
- Who should take action? When and where?
- How should the reader inform you that action will be taken? By when should the reader reply?

I suggest you write no more than three to five paragraphs per email. Make sure to clearly state your business purpose in the opening paragraph of each email message. End with conclusions that spell out what action you plan to take or expect the recipient to take—who does what by when, where and/or how? Use the proper tone in relation to the message and your audience—CEO to CEO.

Determine your business purpose for each case study. Outline and write your email before you read the Widget and Trinket email messages in Appendix Two.

Chapter 7: Email Subject Lines; Hi/Bye; Reply

When it comes to email, the subject line is your first opportunity to catch the reader's attention. Fail to do that and the reader might not open your email message or might not open it in a timely manner. You goal is to speak to your reader and to convey a sense of your purpose.

With that in mind, which subject line do you feel is most effective?

1. Need to meet
2. <Project Name> Meeting, Dec. 14
3. Cost overrun
4. <Project Name> cost overrun prevention

Most people agree, it's number 2. Look at what it contains: what and when. The what is a meeting on <project name>. The when is Dec. 14. You outline your W5 even before you write your subject line so that you can include the most important elements in it. For the sake of this email, we have to presume you are involved in <Project Name>, so the name immediately captures your attention. In addition, you know what is happening (the meeting) and when it is scheduled to take place. So in theory, you don't even have to read the email to book the date for the meeting—the purpose of the email. You are, of course, inclined to read the email because it concerns something that you are involved in.

Let's look at a few more subject lines. Which subject is most specific?

1. Report ready
2. Please read ABC Report
3. ABC Report: feedback required
4. ABC Report feedback due Apr. 21
5. Send feedback on ABC report ASAP

I think you'd agree that it's number 4. By asking for feedback you imply that the report must be read—two birds with one stone, so to speak. By naming the report, you speak to your reader (who we will presume is involved in or interested in the ABC Report). Also, notice that in six words we let the reader know what he has to do and by when he has to do it. If I (the reader) am not able to make this deadline, I can email you. If the deadline is approaching, I can schedule some time to read the report and give you feedback. In other words, based on the subject line alone I can help you achieve your purpose or reason for writing.

Take a look at this subject line:

Report: Focus on Healthcare: Are Canadians Missing an Opportunity?

You know the email contains a report, and what the report is about—healthcare opportunities for Canadians. If you are interested in the topic, you click and read. But what if you started to read the report and saw the following lines off the top:

> In analyzing the growth of the furniture market in the U.S., ABC Research has put a greater emphasis on products that cater to the healthcare furniture industry. ABC Research estimates the annual U.S. market for furniture in the healthcare industry to be about $1.7 billion.

All of the sudden, you see that the report is not about healthcare but about furniture in the healthcare industry. In short, the report is not living up to expectations created by the subject line. So you stop reading. But what of those potential readers who were interested in furniture in the healthcare industry? Most of them have probably not opened the email, let alone started to read the report, because of the misleading subject line that says nothing about furniture.

In other words, take a moment and think about the expectations that this subject line raises. Based on this subject line (or title, if it's the title of a report) you expect the report to focus on healthcare, not healthcare furniture. You read and quickly abandon the report when you realize it's not of interest to you, or you don't read it because the subject line makes it seem like the report is not of interest to you. Who suffers? The writer who has failed to attract readers to the email or report and the people who would actually be interested in the subject. That's how important your subject line is.

If you take a moment and spell out your W5 (think before you write) you are far more likely to use the right words in your subject line—the words that would motivate the right people to read your email for the right reasons. So think before you write: it benefits both the writer and the reader.

Changing the subject line

Email messages can fly back and forth at breakneck speed. Often two people start communicating about one topic and, as emails travel back and forth, they move on to other topics.

If the subject of your email message changes after a couple of replies, change the subject line to reflect the change of topic. This will make it easier for you to file and track down email messages related to particular topics. You can keep the old subject line in brackets as you change subject lines to let the reader know you are continuing an old discussion but addressing a new topic.

Original email subject:

How to write email messages

As you write, the topic of your message changes to how to reply to email messages, so change the subject line:

Replying to email (Was: How to write email messages)

How to start/end email messages

A number of people have asked me how to start and end email messages. The short answer is, it depends. Let's look at some options. Do you start your email with:

- Hi,
- Hi <first name>,
- Hi <last name>,
- Dear <first name>,
- Dear Mr./Ms. <last name>:

First off, email messages are less formal than business letters. If you are writing a letter and you don't know the person you are writing, you would start it like this:

Dear Mr. Smith:

If you know the person, you can start it like this:

Dear Chris,

When it comes to email, here's where the salutation depends. To whom are you writing? How well do you know the person? If you are writing a potential client, someone you have never communicated with before, you might want to start your message with Dear Mr./Ms. <last name>. At the same time, if this person is expecting to hear from you, even if you don't know the person well, you might start it with Hi <first name>. If the person is someone who works for the same company you work for, you might start it with Hi. And if the person is someone you email on a regular basis, you might not have any salutation. You might simply plunge into your message. Simply put, there is no hard and fast rule.

I know people who say that plunging in feels rude. If you feel that way, start your email with Hi, or Hi <first name> or perhaps Good morning or Good afternoon. None of the above is incorrect; what you use depends on how well you know the person and how formal your message is (more on formal and informal tone later).

If you are replying to someone, starting your message is a lot easier—simply mimic the way the writer started the message. If the writer wrote Hi, then you can too. If the writer wrote Dear Ms. <last name>, you can reply using a similar salutation. If you want to let the writer know it's okay to be less formal, you might reply with Hi <first name>. In short, it all depends on what you want to achieve.

If you are using a Blackberry or some other smart phone, typing away with your thumbs, you might simply plunge into your message. But pause first and think before you write: think of who you are writing to and your relationship with that person. If it makes sense, work your thumbs a little harder and type Hi <first name> or some other appropriate salutation.

In short, if you are not sure what to do, answering the following questions should help you decide:

- How well do you know the person?
- How formal or informal is the message?
- Are you sending a quick email reminder or are you sending something similar to a business letter?
- If you have no salutation, how will the reader feel?
- How has the reader addressed you previously?

On the other hand, if your organization has a formal policy about how you should begin email messages, especially when writing to customers or suppliers, follow the policy.

The same rules apply to ending email, with some exceptions. First off, do you end your emails with:

- Regards,
- Sincerely,
- Cheers,

Do you use your first name or first and last names?

Again, it depends. How well do you know the person? If not well, or if you are writing a formal email message, you would use something like this:

Regards,
Paul Lima

If you were writing a friend, you might use Cheers, or Cheers <first name>. If you were writing to someone inside your company that you communicated with on a regular basis, you might not even sign your message (after all, your name is in the "from" field, so the recipient knows who is sending the email).

Now here is where signing off gets more complicated. Do you want this person to have your website, email address and phone number? Are there any legalities you should address in your sign off? I'd suggest that the latter should be a company decision. You know the kind of thing you see below signatures in email you might receive from an insurance or an accounting firm:

> This communication is intended for use by the individual(s) to whom it is specifically addressed and should not be read by, or delivered to, any other person. Such communication may contain privileged or confidential information. If you have received this communication in error, please notify the sender and permanently delete the communication. Thank you for your cooperation.

I find such disclaimers overkill. However, if your company has a signature and/or a disclaimer policy, then you need to follow it. Email messages are official company communications and can be referred to in case of legal action or other disputes. So follow company protocol when sending and replying to email. In short, if your company needs to use a disclaimer like the one above, then everybody who sends email outside the company should use the disclaimer. In many cases, it is automatically added to email messages by the company servers so there's nothing for you to be concerned about.

If I am writing clients or prospects, and I want them to be able to get to my website quickly or call me if they need to without having to search for my phone number, I use a longer, more formal, signature:

> Regards,
> Paul Lima
> Phone: (416) 628-6005
> Email: info@paullima.com
> Web: www.paullima.com

At the risk of sounding like a broken record, think before you sign off and use the signature that is most appropriate for the circumstances.

Replying to email

I've had people ask me if they should use the W5 when replying to email messages. I always answer their questions with one of my own, "Do you want to be an effective email writer?" If they answer my question in the affirmative, I then answer their original question in the affirmative. After all, what are your options? Hit reply and start typing madly? Or take a moment to think before you write? If you want to be effective, I suspect you will agree that you should think before you write.

At the same time, if I invite you to a specific meeting at a specific place at a specific date and time and ask you to reply, your reply could be as short as this:

I'll be there.

In other words, the sender does not need any more information than that. On the other hand, if I gave you date and time options, I'd expect a reply that contained a bit more information:

I can attend the meeting on January 15 at 2 pm.

In other words, your reply depends in large part on what the sender needs to close the communication loop. However, when sending a more complex reply, you want to use the W5 to create your reply outline and allude to your purpose in the opening paragraph. In other words, after you answer the W5 questions, review your answers and put them in logical order. Write your email from point to point. Edit and revise as may be necessary. Proofread. Send.

Are there ways to shorten the process when replying? Considering that it might take you only a moment or two to go through the process, I'd suggest that you not take any shortcuts. If you leave out any important information, the entire process will take more time than it should because the person you replied to will have to ask for clarification and you'll have to reply again. Or the person you replied to will misunderstand your message and something important might fall through the cracks.

Adding to the reply process

In fact, I'd like to add to the process. When I receive an important or complex email message, I copy it, hit reply and paste it in the reply area. I reread it and outline my W5 below the message I've pasted into the reply space.

Once that is done, I write my reply by editing the original message—eliminating anything that I do not have to address and revising anything I need to reply to. In short, I use the original message as a template for my reply. It's as if the original message is a stone block from which I sculpt my reply. But I also outline my W5 so that I can add information, as may be required, as I reply to the original message. Of course, before I hit send, I review my reply and make any necessary edits.

There is a certain irony here. The better written the original message, the more effective my reply. In other words, if the original message is effective and comprehensive, I tend not to have to pull in anything from my W5 work. With that in mind, allow me to summarize this reply process:
- Read the original message.
- Copy the original message.
- Hit reply (you will see the original message below an *original message* line).

- Paste the copied original message above the original message line.
- Jot down answers to W5, in relation to the original message, beneath the original message.
- Sculpt your reply out of the original message and add any pertinent details from your W5 points.
- Edit/proofread your reply and send.

Note: This method may not work for Blackberries, iPhones and other smart phones. However, the same principle applies. Make sure you respond to the salient points raised in the original message while adding additional points based on your W5 thinking.

Avoid the >> reply

Why do I copy the original message and then compose over it, instead of simply replying to various elements of the original message under those elements?

One of your goals in writing is to be clear. When you reply to various elements of a message by writing under each of those elements, clarity can suffer. Imagine if a message goes back and forth several times and both writers reply below lines in the original message. Soon you could be looking at this:

```
> I agree with what you're saying, and believe
> we can work together to resolve the issue.
> I too have a few concerns about who should
> take the lead on this one. Let's kick it up the
> ladder and see what Tom thinks.
>> This is something that needs to be resolved
>> quickly if we are going to avoid serious issues
>> down the road with our staff and how they
>> interact with our customers by email. I am
>> willing to address the issue but wonder if a
>> formal policy should be issued by someone
>> higher up.
>>> Last week I heard from one of our regular
>>> customers about an inappropriate email he
>>> received from a service rep he has been
>>> working with for several years. I guess the
>>> rep presumed they were friends and felt
>>> comfortable sharing the material with the
>>> customer. We should take action. But what
>>> action and who should take it?
```

In some cases, primarily with the use of formatted email, replies are indented and older replies are reduced in type size. Such messages can be incredibly difficult to read:

> I agree with what you're saying, and believe
> we can work together to resolve the issue.
> I too have a few concerns about who should
> take the lead on this one. Let's kick it up the
> ladder and see what Tom thinks.
>> This is something that needs to be resolved
>> quickly if we are going to avoid serious
>> issues down the road with our staff and how
>> they interact with our customers by email. I
>> am willing to address the issue but wonder if
>> a formal policy should be issued by someone
>> higher up.
>>> Last week I heard from one of our
>>> regular customers about an inappropriate
>>> email he received from a service rep he has
>>> been working with for several years. I guess
>>> the rep presumed they were friends and felt
>>> comfortable sharing the material with the
>>> customer. We should take action. But what
>>> action and who should take it?

In addition, imagine if either of the above messages is then sent to someone with a note that says, "We need your feedback on this issue." The poor person has to struggle through the now convoluted email and try to make heads or tails of it before he or she can reply.

I'm sure you've seen even more convoluted email than the ones above. In short, you are better off reading the message, clicking reply and replying in full, just as if you were composing an original message. Also, if the message has to be forwarded to a third party at some point, you are better off forwarding a series of clearly written messages rather than a series of convoluted indents and >>> lines. In other words, you want to forward a clear, concise, cohesive message to the third party, not a so-called dog's breakfast.

Auto-Reply

Email seems to be everywhere. Mobile email devices, such as the BlackBerry and iPhone, mean many people cannot get away from it. There may be times when you need to take some downtime from email. And there may be times when you simply cannot access your email. If you are in a meeting or otherwise out of touch, use auto-reply (if your email system allows you to do so) to let senders know that your reply will be delayed. You might even be able to use auto-reply to answer the types of questions you normally get or to provide the kind of information you frequently provide.

When you use auto-reply, senders get an automatically generated message that informs them that you are out of the office. Most auto-reply systems let you compose the email message that senders will receive. Take some time to think about who might be emailing you and what they might need—especially if you are dealing with customers or other people who are not part of your organization. In your auto-reply message:

- acknowledge receipt of the email
- let the sender know when you'll be back or otherwise able to reply
- if someone is covering for you while you are away, include that person's name, email address and phone number

However, you might want to go beyond the basics in your auto-reply message. You might want to cover a few other work-related points. For instance, you might want to add a short FAQ (answers to frequently asked questions) to your standard auto-reply message, although you do not need to use the FAQ question and answer format. Your reply might include lines as simple as these:

- If you need information about <subject>, please contact <name, contact information>.
- If you are concerned about delivery of <item>, please contact <name, contact information>.
- If this is a customer service issue, please contact <name, contact information>.

Of course, depending on the nature of your typical email communication, your auto-reply can include much more information. Whatever you include, you want your readers to understand that they are receiving an auto-reply and to know what their options are. In short, you still want your reply to be as clear, concise and focused as possible.

Chapter 8: Email Etiquette

I want to spend a bit of time looking at some basic email writing etiquette. Let's start with one thing that bugs me: people using CC (carbon copy) or Bcc (blind carbon copy) as if they were running a covert operation. I am not saying you should never use Cc or Bcc; I'm just saying think about it first and then make it a conscious decision. But let's start at the beginning.

To, Cc and Bcc

When you email someone, you enter the person's email address in the To field. If you want to send an email message to several people, you can enter all of their email addresses in the To field. However, if you have primary and secondary contacts, you can enter the email address of the primary contact in the To field and enter the email addresses of the secondary contacts in the Cc field.

The primary contact is usually a person (or persons) who must reply or take action. Those who receive the email message as a Cc often receive it as an FYI (for your information). However, they might have to take action based on the content of the email message. Make sure you are clear about who should do what.

Think twice about using Cc in an email message to a large group of people. If someone receives an email message as a Cc and hits reply-to-all, the reply goes to all the people who received the original email message. If you do not want all the people on the list to receive replies, that can be an issue. In your message, you might want to let the recipients of your email know that they should not rely to all.

In addition, when you Cc a group, you expose all the email addresses of the people who received your message. This is not a problem if the group does not mind. However, if you do not want to expose email addresses, and/or if you do not want the people you have emailed to receive replies, use Bcc.

If you send an email message to a primary contact and send it Bcc to others, the person in the To field, and those in the Bcc field, cannot reply-to-all and will not be able to see the names and email addresses of those you sent the message to as a Bcc. In fact, the person you sent the email to won't even know that you have sent it Bcc to others unless you tell him. Bcc is often used when you are engaged in a sticky situation or one that is political and you want to copy someone without letting the primary contact know that you have sent the email message to another or to others. However, you can also use Bcc and let the person in the To field know that you have sent the email message to other recipients using Bcc for their information or to update them on the stats of a project.

Again, people often over-use Cc and Bcc because it's easy to do. Your organization might have rules about when and when not to use Cc and Bcc. If not, it might want to implement such rules. In the meantime, you can reduce the amount of email you send by thinking about who really needs to see what you have to say. If a large group of people need to read your message, then Cc and Bcc are there for you to use.

To format or not to format?

There was, for a while, a big debate over the use of formatted and plain text email. If you send an email in plain text, you cannot control the font (also known as typeface) or text size or color. Formatted email messages, on the other hand, let you:

- Use different typestyles and different fonts, such as Times, Arial or **Broadway**. I suggest you avoid fancy, difficult-to-read fonts (such as Broadway), unless you are creating something creative.
- Use different type sizes. I suggest you stick with one type size (generally 10 to 12 point), unless you are embedding a report in your email and want to use a larger type size for your title and subheads. On the other hand, it is better to use Word or Acrobat (PDF files) for reports and attach them to your email.
- Use different colors, **bold**, *italic* and <u>underline</u>. You may want to use a second color to emphasize a particular point; however, use additional colors (as well as bold, italic and underline) sparingly. Fancy formatting may actually interfere with the clarity of your communication; however, *judicious* use of bold (or other formats) can help you emphasize a point.
- Embed images, graphics, icons or smileys ☺. I suggest you do not use smileys and that you keep the embedding of images or graphics to a minimum. Again, use Word or PDFs if you have to send a message with images, charts or graphics.

In short, if you use formatted email, use black type (one font, one size) on a white background, with no or few images. Use bold judiciously on subheads in a longer email message. You can also use bullets and numbering if you want to convey a list of facts or ideas. Beyond that, keep your formatting simple. Let your writing and tone clearly communicate what you are saying, instead of your formatting. In addition, keep in mind that your email message might be forwarded to other recipients. Ask yourself how you would feel if someone you did not know received a message that you composed, and it was full of smileys. I bet you'd feel like this: ☹

Beware of the TLA*

You may use acronyms in email, as long as you are sure your readers understand what you mean. However, I suggest you spell out the name in full followed by the acronym in brackets, as in Canadian Medical Association (CMA). The next time you refer to the association in your message, you can use CMA. By way of aside, CMA also stands for Chartered Management Accounts, Canadian Marketing Association and several other organizations. So using the name in full in your message ensures there will be no confusion.

*TLA is the three-letter acronym for Three Letter Acronym. If I used TLA in an email without first using the full name I would, no doubt, confuse most readers.

Brief and to the point

Keep messages brief and to the point. Your writing may be grammatically correct but if your message is not concise and focused, you risk having your reader give up on your message. So concentrate on concise, focused writing. Using W5 to outline what you want to write before you write it will help you achieve that.

AVOID ALL CAPS

When writing, use sentence case as opposed to USING ALL CAPITAL LETTERS, which looks like you are SHOUTING. using all lowercase letters, on the other hand, looks lazy. Avoid all lower case too.

Talk to people

In a globally connected world, it's too easy to use email as an excuse to avoid personal contact. There is value in face-to-face or voice-to-voice communication. The higher the financial or emotional stakes, the more important it is that you talk to someone. At the beginning of a complex process, talk first to ensure everybody understands what has to be done and why. Then you can use email to keep people informed, for status updates or for minor troubleshooting.

Email is not private

Many people treat email communication as they would a private whisper. If, however, you are emailing someone from your work email address, your communication is not private. It is company property. It resides on the company email server and can be viewed by appropriate people or used in legal matters. Keep that in mind when you are emailing.

Chapter 9: Constructing Sentences

In the beginning was the word. It was quickly followed by the sentence. Which, of course, was followed by the paragraph.

Do you know what the shortest sentence in the Bible is? Two words: *Jesus wept.* The sentence has a subject (*Jesus*) and a verb (*wept*). That is all a sentence needs to be complete. Where, however, is the subject in the following two-word sentence?

> Do it!

The subject, *you*, in a command or imperative is understood. Everyone who hears the simple command *Do it!* understands it to mean <u>*You*</u> *do it*. Drop the *you*, start the sentence with the verb (to do), and the sentence packs a more powerful punch.

Without a subject (real or implied) and verb, you have a sentence fragment:

> Because I.
> Over there.
> The officer.

However, look at the third sentence in this chapter:

> Which, of course, was followed by the paragraph.

When you read it, did you notice that it was a sentence fragment? (Where is the subject?) Did it feel like a fragment when you read it? Even if it did, was it effective? Does it feel like a fragment now that you are reading it out of context? Although sentence fragments can be used effectively, particularly in advertising, seldom will you use them in business writing. If they aren't used appropriately—to emphasize a particular point, for instance—they can create disjointed writing and cause miscommunication and confusion.

Part of your goal as a business writer is to become aware of, and correct, sentence faults and other problems that can interfere with clear, concise communication. You do this when editing your work. In other words, don't get hung up on fixing errors as you write. That will thwart your writing efficiency. At the same time, if you follow the writing process, especially the creation of detailed outlines, you will bring greater clarity and focus to your writing and have fewer revisions to make when editing.

While grammar and spelling count, this is not a book about grammar and spelling and I will not spend much time on particular grammatical faults. We will look at the active and passive voice and how to construct effective sentences in this chapter. However, if grammar is an issue for you, you should look for other books (there are too many out there, not to mention online resources) to help you.

Active versus passive voice

Read the two passages below. What is different about them? What is similar?

> The Highway Department is building a new bridge in River Hollow. The backhoe digs deep holes. The cement mixer pours in concrete to make the supports.
>
> Carefully Carlton picks up steel girders with his crane and lays them across the supports.
>
> Bulldozers push up the surrounding ground to make a road. The grading machine smoothes the slope, and the asphalt spreader pours down a layer of blacktop. Brian's steamroller comes last to smooth it flat and even. Dennis and Darlene haul away the extra dirt in their dump truck.

■ ■ ■

> Research into new advertising promotions that could boost company sales was initiated by marketing last spring.
>
> A list of primary media read by our target market was compiled by Susan McMillan. Creative ideas were produced by the copywriting department. A campaign was designed by Frank Myers, the art director, and was launched in the summer.
>
> Encouraging have been the sales results to date.

Does the first passage remind you of a grade one reader? If you are old enough to have gone on adventures with Dick and Jane, it might remind you of those famous sentences that you read when you were first learning to read:

> See Dick. See Jane. See Dick run. See Jane run. See Spot. See Spot run. Hear Spot bark.

The sentences above are clear enough, but are they effective or are they boring and monotonous? Could you imagine reading an entire report with sentences written only like the ones in the first or the second passage above?

In the first passage, the simple sentences are written in the active voice, which can be used to create short, direct sentences. The second passage is written entirely in the passive voice, which makes for longer, more awkward sentences that distance the reader from who did what.

While effective sentences are generally written in the active voice, effective writing requires a mix of active and passive voice, a mix of complex and simple sentences and the use of sentences of various lengths.

Active voice

In the active voice, the *subject* performs the action expressed by the **verb**. In other words, the subject acts, as in these examples:

> The dog **bit** the boy.

> Terri **presented** her research at the conference.

> We **received** your shipment two days late, which caused delays.

> You **sent** the shipment two days late, which caused delays.

> Scientists **will conduct** experiments to test the hypothesis.

Passive voice

In the passive voice, the *subject* receives the action expressed by the **verb**. The agent performing the action may appear in a "by the..." phrase or may be omitted entirely.

> The boy **was bitten** by the dog.

> Research **was presented** by Terri at the conference.

> Your payment **was received** two days late, which caused delays.

> Experiments **will be conducted** to test the hypothesis.

Notice the agents committing the action are missing from the last two sentences. Here are the last two sentences with the "by the" agents included:

> Your payment was received two days late by the accounting department, which caused delays.

> Experiments will be conducted by the scientists to test the hypothesis.

Do you need "by the accounting department" or "by the scientists" in the above sentences? The sentences are grammatically correct without the agents. If, however, it was important for the reader to know that the accounting department did not receive the payments, or that scientists will conduct the experiments, then the agents should be included. If not, you can leave them out.

Leaving the scientists out of the second sentence puts the focus on the experiments and why they will be conducted. There is nothing wrong with this focus, if that is where you want to put it. In other words, where you put your emphasis or focus, and the voice you use, should be conscious decisions.

Having said that, you should know that the passive voice can create awkward sentences and cause readers to become confused. Sentences written in the active voice require fewer words than those written in the passive voice. This makes for writing that is more concise. In addition, sentences in the active voice are generally clearer and more direct than those in the passive voice.

The passive voice can allow writers to compose without using personal pronouns or names of people or groups (as with the scientists and accounting department sentences). This can help create the appearance of an objective, fact-based discourse. However, the passive voice can also be used to deflect blame or avoid responsibility, which is not always warranted, as in the following sentence:

> Seeking to lay off workers without taking the blame, consultants were hired to break the bad news.

Who was seeking to lay off workers? The consultants? That's what it looks like. However, the CEO was more likely responsible. If that is the case, leaving out the agent creates a misleading sentence that avoids allocating proper responsibility. So let's use active voice and include the responsible party:

> Seeking to lay off workers without taking the blame, the CEO hired consultants to break the bad news.

Being direct can be important. There are times, however, when being indirect is preferable. If there is no clear agent, then there is no clear blame, and sometimes it is necessary to point out a problem without pointing fingers, as in these examples:

> Several mistakes were made before the trains collided.

> The quota was not met last month, so monthly bonuses have been withheld.

In the train example, imagine that a train collision is under review. It is obvious that the trains should not have collided. The spokesperson for the railway company cannot deny that a collision has occurred. However, the spokesperson cannot say who made the mistakes that caused the collision until the accident review is completed. Instead, she resorts to the passive voice and leaves out the agent so she does not allocate blame. If she had included the agent, she might have said something like this:

> Several mistakes were made by the eastbound engineer before the trains collided.

And if she had used the active voice, she might have said this:

> The eastbound engineer made several mistakes before the trains collided.

In the quota example, the person making the announcement might know which person or department did not meet quota but has chosen not to say it publicly. Also, notice that the person making the announcement has not credited an individual—the CFO (chief financial officer) or a specific manager—for withholding bonuses. What we have here is the withholding of two agents and the double use of the passive voice in one sentence, but it is not necessarily doublespeak. You might call it politically sensitive communication. Put in the agents and what do you have?

> The quota was not met last month by the western sales team, so monthly bonuses have been withheld by the CFO.

How does the western sales team feel? What do people think about the CFO?

Choosing active or passive voice

Since the passive voice highlights what is acted upon rather than focusing on the agent performing the action, using it often makes sense when the agent performing the action is obvious, unknown or unimportant. It also makes sense when a writer wishes to postpone mentioning the agent until the last part of the sentence, or to avoid mentioning the agent. In the active voice, the agent or subject is important, or integral, to the sentence.

In the examples below, the passive voice makes sense if the agent is less important than the action and what is acted upon. If the agent is important, one would use the active voice.

> **Active**: The dispatcher notified police only minutes after three prisoners had escaped.

> **Passive**: Police were notified only minutes after three prisoners had escaped.

If it is more important to know how long it took the police to be notified than it is to know who notified the police, the passive voice makes sense. If there was some question as to who notified the police, and if that was important, the active voice would make sense.

What is more important in these sentences? The spruce budworm or the damage?

> **Active**: The spruce budworm has irrevocably damaged vast expanses of Cape Breton forests.
>
> **Passive**: Vast expanses of Cape Breton forests have been irrevocably damaged by the spruce budworm.

In the passive voice sentence, the emphasis is on the damage to the forests, not the cause of the damage. If, however, you wanted to warn people about the spruce budworm, the active voice would make more sense.

When choosing between the active and passive voice, what you want to do is keep the reader, your topic and your purpose in mind. Also, think about clarity and conciseness. In other words, make conscious decisions concerning the use of the active and passive voice and the inclusion or exclusion of the agent performing the action. However, beware of using the passive voice to mask issues that should be addressed and don't overuse the passive voice.

Convert passive to active

Take a moment and convert the passive voice sentences below to active voice. If you are not sure that you have done it correctly, use the grammar checker in your word processing software to flag passive voice and grammar check your revised sentences. You can also look at the revised sentences in Appendix Three.

> The entrance exam was failed by more than one third of the applicants to the school.
>
> The brakes were slammed on by her as the car sped downhill.
>
> Your bicycle has been damaged.
> (*The agent has been omitted. Who did the damage? Edit the sentence as if you did and edit it as if a thief has damaged the bicycle.*)
>
> Action on the bill is being considered by the committee.
>
> By then, the soundtrack will have been completely remixed by the sound engineers.
>
> To satisfy the instructor's demands for legibility, the paper was written on a computer.

(Before revising this, ask yourself the following: Who was satisfying the instructor? The paper? Or the person writing the paper? Then edit the sentence.)

Once you have converted passive sentences to active, continue to read.

How to construct a sentence

I want to take a moment to review the foundation of the sentence. At minimum, the sentence requires a subject and a verb (action). In *I laughed*, *I* is the subject; *laughed* is the verb. But two-word sentences generally don't cut it in business writing. So let's review a sentence that includes a *subject*, a **verb** and a third component—the object.

The boy **kicked** <u>the soccer ball</u>.

The boy is our subject (person who does the action). **Kicked** is the verb (action). <u>The soccer ball</u> is our object—receives action. I call these three elements "the heart of the sentence." If you ever feel that your sentences are getting too complex, find the heart. Once you have the heart, you can expand your sentence logically and keep the meaning clear. For instance, where did the ball go when the boy kicked it?

The boy kicked the soccer ball through the window.

What happened to the window?

The boy kicked the soccer ball through the window, which shattered into a thousand pieces.

Tell me more about this boy:

The tall, thin, Caucasian boy kicked the soccer ball through the window, which shattered into a thousand pieces.

Do you see how our sentence is becoming more complex? It is easy to understand, however, because we can still identify the heart of the sentence. Now imagine that a criminal committed this action.

The tall, thin, armed and dangerous Caucasian boy kicked the soccer ball through the window, which shattered into a thousand pieces, and then he fled the scene.

Notice we now have two "hearts" combined. Let me simplify them for you:

The boy kicked the soccer ball through the window.

He fled the scene.

Two subjects, two verbs, two objects. One sentence. Meaning is still clear because we let one heart beat, so to speak, and then the other. However, if you think sentences are running away on you, identify your subject and verb and build from there. If you have more than one subject and verb, identify each of them and determine how best to let them beat, either joined in one sentence or as two separate sentences. If the complex sentence feels like it is unclear, separate the two hearts:

> The tall, thin, armed and dangerous Caucasian boy kicked the soccer ball through the window, which shattered into a thousand pieces. Then he fled the scene.

Keep this in mind as you try the other writing exercises in this book and as you write and edit your work.

Chapter 10: Creating Paragraphs

A paragraph is a collection of sentences organized around a clearly defined topic. If you are writing a long document, each paragraph topic will be a subtopic of, or somehow related to, the subject of the document you are writing.

The paragraph performs three functions:
1. develops the unit of thought stated in the topic sentence
2. provides a logical break in the material
3. creates a visual break on the page, thus signaling a new topic

Generally, the paragraph starts with a topic sentence. Often, this topic sentence is an important outline point converted into a complete sentence, followed by your subtopic outline points. The topic sentence states the paragraph's main idea. The rest of the paragraph supports and develops the idea.

The topic sentence is often the first sentence in a paragraph because it tells the reader what the paragraph is about. However, the topic sentence can be used to end a paragraph—almost like a punch line. Occasionally, the topic sentence can be found in the middle of the paragraph. There would be some build up to the topic sentence, the topic sentence and then some support of the topic.

Topic at the beginning

Here is an example with the topic sentence at the beginning of each paragraph:

The cost of orientation, health and safety and customer service training for new Customer Service Representatives (CSRs) is significant. The organization must cover the price of classroom facilities, instructors and manuals, and must pay employees their full salary during the two-week training period.

If the company is to break even on its training, employees must stay on the job for at least one year, according to our analysis (see attached PDF). However, on average, CSRs leave the company within nine months of hiring. Not only is the company losing money on employee training, it is also paying exorbitant recruitment costs to fill each vacancy.

To increase the training return on investment (ROI), we propose that the following recommendations be implemented:

1. Recommendation one....
2. Recommendation two....
3. Recommendation three....

Notice how the first sentence of the first paragraph establishes both the subject of the document as well as the topic of the paragraph: "The cost of… is significant." I suspect you could imagine this sentence being used to establish the topic in almost any paragraph dealing with cost issues, such as: *The cost of purchasing parts from our current supplier is significant.* In short, the sentence raises an issue. This creates expectations that the document will explain why the cost is significant and might even suggest how the issue can be resolved.

The opening sentence of the second paragraph tells us the circumstances that must occur if we are to solve the problem. "If the company is to break even on its investment in training, employees must stay in the job for which they have been hired for at least one year, according to our analysis (see attached PDF)."

It often makes sense to attach complex details to an email message or to include them in an appendix of a report. By attaching the PDF, the writer can move quickly from the problem to the solution while offering skeptics, or those who need more information, proof in the attached document or report appendix.

Finally, notice how the third paragraph consists of a topic sentence and five points or the actions to be taken. (There will be more on when and why to use bullet points or numbered lists later in this chapter.) The document does not say when to take the action nor does it request feedback to close the communication loop. Presumably, the writers are sending this information to management. Management must decide what to do and when to do it, not the writers, so the writers do not have to request that action be taken by a specific date.

Topic at the end

Here is an example with the topic sentence at the end of the paragraph:

> Energy does more than simply make our lives more comfortable and convenient. If you wanted to reverse or stop economic progress, the surest way to do so would be to cut off the nation's oil resources. The country would plummet into the abyss of economic ruin. *In short, our economy is energy-based.*

Often—not always—opening paragraphs in email messages, letters, executive summaries of reports and other documents place the topic sentence at the end of the paragraph. This lets the writer set the stage with a few lines that build up to the topic or purpose of the document.

Your topic and purpose can be made clear in the first line of the first paragraph, the last line of the first paragraph or even part way through your first paragraph. The important thing is that, almost without exception, the reader needs to know what you are writing about (your topic) and why (your purpose) by the end of the opening paragraph.

Paragraph length

Although this is not a book about layout and design, you need to know that the look of your document can affect the attitude of readers toward your writing—even before they begin to read your document (or perhaps not read it, if the writing looks like an impenetrable wall of words). For instance, how would you react if you received an email, or any document, with paragraphs that looked like this one:

> In analyzing the growth of the furniture market in the U.S., ABC Research has put a greater emphasis on products that cater to the healthcare furniture industry. ABC Research estimates the annual U.S. market for furniture in the healthcare industry to be about $1.7 billion. This outstrips the growth of other furniture markets, such as the business and home markets. Most of the healthcare furniture market is supplied by regional suppliers. The overall healthcare furniture market is split 50/50 between traditional office furniture and clinical furniture suppliers. ABC indicated that the market is expected to grow by 50% over the next seven years, driven by an aging population and the need to replace aging healthcare facilities. Expectations of ABC are that there will be a greater growth within the clinical segment of the healthcare furniture market. Although Canadian furniture manufacturers have talked about focusing on end markets in the U.S. including government, education and healthcare, U.S. manufacturers have made more significant investments in targeting the healthcare furniture market. They are offering clinical products that complement their traditional office furniture products. Given the expected growth in the market, Canadian manufacturers that want to break into the U.S. healthcare furniture market should acquire small U.S. furniture suppliers with heavy healthcare exposure as a way to increase penetration into this market.

I suspect you would have a negative reaction. You would want to see several paragraphs to break up this wall of words. In other words, even before you read this document, you are reacting in a negative manner. You might even postpone reading this document simply because of the way it looks.

So how long should paragraphs be?

The length of each paragraph should aid the reader's understanding of the idea expressed. It's that simple. A series of very short paragraphs, just like the wall of words above, can indicate poor organization. Too many short paragraphs can also indicate an underdeveloped thought process, just as overly long paragraphs can fail to provide the reader with manageable subdivisions of thought.

The occasional one-sentence paragraph is acceptable if it is used for effect or as a transition between paragraphs.

Paragraph exercise

Take a shot at editing the long paragraph presented above. Your goal is to read it, understand it, determine your purpose, organize it (create an outline) and revise it.

If you believe there is more than one topic addressed in the paragraph, turn it into multiple paragraphs. Rewrite sentences. Delete any information that does not advance your purpose. Create clear, concise writing that captures attention, holds interest, influences attitude and presents a clear call to action based on the facts.

There is a sample of a revised wall of words in Appendix Four. However, tackle this exercise before you read it. Give your internal editor a good workout. And do not be concerned if your take on the paragraph is not the same as the example. No two people would produce the same revised document. The example is simply how one editor would turn the long paragraph into a more concise, focused, well-structured message.

Once you have revised the long paragraph above, continue to read.

Bullet points and numbered lists

As we saw previously in this chapter, in the topic sentence example about "the cost of orientation, health and safety and customer service training," there are times when bullet points or numbered lists make sense.

Bullet points and numbered lists are easy to scan and absorb. They make sense when you are making a series of recommendations or when you are giving instructions—especially if the instructions must be performed sequentially. The examples below are presented as conventional paragraphs and then as lists. In the first example, you have to take the steps in sequential order, hence the numbered list. In the second example, you should follow the points presented but you don't have to follow them sequentially, hence the bullet points.

Example I

For you to start juggling, do the following: first pick up A in your right hand, then you should pick up B in you left hand, and then you should toss A and then B into the air, catching A as you toss B and catching B and you toss A. Repeat continuously.

For you to start juggling, do the following:
1. pick up A in your right hand
2. pick up B in your left hand
3. toss A into the air
4. toss B into the air while catching A

5. toss A back into the air while catching B
6. repeat continuously

◨ ◨ ◨

Example II

Three habits that improve health are getting eight hours of sleep each night, eating three balanced meals every day and exercising regularly.

Three habits that improve health are:
- getting eight hours of sleep each night
- eating three balanced meals every day
- exercising regularly

The points convey the information in a manner that is easy to scan, absorb and understand. The shorter lines cause the eye to stop at the end of each point as the brain does a mental check. Then the eye moves to the beginning of the next point and repeats the pattern. Look for opportunities to use bullet or numbered points in your work. However, don't overdo it. A page full of points can look almost as tedious to read as the wall-of-words presented earlier in this chapter.

In addition:
- Bullet points used for no reason don't make sense.
- If you use them just because you think you should
- You could confuse the reader.
- The reader will be looking for a list of instructions or recommendations
- Where none exists.
- That can be confusing.
- Enough said, yes?

Chapter 11: Toning Up Your Writing

Tone is the attitude a writer expresses toward the subject and his or her readers. You demonstrate tone through the word and grammar choices you make and the degree of formality or informality of your writing.

What is the difference between the following two headlines or titles?

> The ecological consequences of diminishing water resources in Canada

> What happens when we've drained Canada dry?

Where would you expect to find the first one? Why? Where would you expect to find the second one?

Is it fair to say you might read the second one in a newspaper or magazine? Even though the subject is serious, the tone is light and informal. The headline is trying to capture the attention of a mass market—perhaps people who tend to scan the news. Notice how it plays on the name of the soft drink, Canada Dry. Look at how it uses a contraction—we've—which indicates an informal style. Consider how the title asks a question to engage the reader in a dialogue.

The first title is more formal, perhaps even a bit ponderous. However, you might expect (expectation is key here) to receive a document with this headline if you were an environmental scientist reading a scholarly journal or a minister of the environment receiving a report issued by the head of one of your many departments. You don't expect to be having a conversation with the writer. Rather, you expect to sit back and be informed.

Two truths

When it comes to tone, there are two truths:
1. The tone of business writing should always be professional and meet the expectations of your readers.
2. The expectations of your readers change according to the relationship between you and the reader.

What is the difference in tone between the two email messages below? Which of the two messages is more formal? Why? Which is the least formal? What are the tone indicators? What is the relationship between the sender and the receiver in each message? How does that affect tone?

Hi Steve,

Your proposal for the reply to the Johnson and Gupta request for quote is super. We just need to hammer out the production schedule. It's a tad tight right now. If we get the contract, I owe you lunch.

Cheers,
Jean

◼ ◼ ◼

To: The Bid Committee

The reply to the Johnson and Gupta Request for Quote appears complete, based on our department's evaluation. However, we have made several suggested revisions to the proposed delivery schedule to help ensure the company does not commit itself to an unrealistic production schedule.

The revisions are clearly indicated in the copy of the attached report. If you have any questions or comments, please reply by September 30.

The first message, I think you would agree, is informal. Words and phrases such as *super, hammer out, tad tight* and *owe you lunch* are informal markers. The second message is formal, as indicated by words and phrases such as *appears complete, our department's evaluation, several suggested revisions, to help ensure, are clearly indicated, the attached report,* and *please reply by.*

The writer of the first message, Jean, obviously knows the recipient, Steve. One can presume they are colleagues, even friends. The writer of the second message is representing a department that can only make suggestions; the final reply to the request for quote is up to the Bid Committee. The committee has obviously requested input but it does not have to listen to the suggestions. In short, the tone of the second message is formal and does not take anything for granted, as in *we have made several suggested revisions...*

Technically, there is nothing wrong with the first message; however, it is easy for email messages to be forwarded to others. You should keep that in mind when you write. While an informal tone might be appropriate when you are sending an email message to a friend or to someone you've known for some time, the informal tone might not be appropriate to other readers to whom the email might be forwarded. Also, as mentioned, email messages are legal documents and considered company property. If a dispute or other legal issue occurs, your messages can be reviewed. You want to make sure you haven't said anything inappropriate and you want to ensure your tone is appropriate.

Tone: positive versus negative

Review the two sets of messages below. You should be able to see the difference the use of positive language makes to writing.

> You didn't send us your signed invoice, so we have not yet processed your payment.

> So we can process your payment promptly, please send us your signed invoice.

◨ ◨ ◨

> Your company's lack of preparation in response to the need for full financial disclosure under Sarbanes-Oxley will have a negative impact on investor confidence.

> Preparing for full financial disclosure under Sarbanes-Oxley will greatly boost investor confidence in your company.

The second message in each set uses positive language and the reader would be more likely to respond in a positive manner, as the writer intended. In other words, given the positive benefits presented in each of the second messages, the reader would be more likely to submit an invoice and would be more likely to prepare for full financial disclosure.

You can use negative words and phrases—*not, have not, did not, never*—or words and phrases that convey concepts in a negative manner—*lack of, negative impact*—in business writing; however, conveying your ideas using a positive tone will more often generate the results you want. If a situation is life and death, may lead to an injury or substantial loss or if you have not previously received the results you desired, you might have to resort to a negative tone. However, in general, you should not convey ideas, concepts and requests using negative language. Or as one might say in a more positive manner: *in general, you should convey ideas, concepts and requests using positive language.*

Sometimes language can be positive but still convey a negative tone. The passage below uses positive language; however, the tone is negative. It says, "Go away. Don't bother me. Solve this yourself." Here's the scenario. Upon requesting information by email about financial planning services from your bank, you receive the following reply:

> Your email of December 5 requesting information about the bank's financial planning services has been received. Financial planning services are offered through selected branches. For

information on the bank's financial planning services, you
should contact someone at your local branch and find the
closest branch that offers such services.

How would you feel if you received an email message from your bank like this one? Again, the language is not negative; however, the tone is. It says, "I can't help you; I don't even want to try." On the other hand, the message below uses mostly positive words (it does spell out a negative situation but offers a positive solution) coupled with a positive and helpful tone:

Thank you for your email. Our financial planning services are
offered through selected branches and I forwarded your request
for information to the Roncesvalles and Howard Park branch,
the branch closest to your home.

You should hear from a financial advisor by Monday. If you do
not hear from a financial advisor by then, or if you have any
other questions, please contact me for assistance.

In summary, when writing, strike the right tone—a tone that is appropriate to your audience, topic and situation.

"You" point of view

The use of *you* or *your* (the *you viewpoint*) can be inclusive and even friendly (as it is in the first Johnson and Gupta email message and in the second email reply from the bank). Using *you* can make the reader feel like part of the event, situation, problem or solution. Advertisers often use *you* to make it seem like they are talking to one reader even though the ad appears in a newspaper that will be read by thousands of people. For years, the McDonald's slogan was "You deserve a break today." While *you* can be polite and inclusive, it can also feel like an accusation or a command (in the imperative, as we've seen, the *you* is often implied).

Can you feel the difference in tone between the following?

Help me sort this out.

I need help resolving this.

Can you please help me resolve this?

While the first two lines might get you the help you need, the *you* in the third line, coupled with *please*, makes the request a personal and polite appeal and will more likely get you the requested assistance. Notice, though, that words like *you* and *your* are not used in the second Johnson and Gupta email. The email message could have been written like this:

Your Johnson and Gupta proposal appears complete and thorough, based on our department's evaluation. Several small revisions to your document, however, would ensure that you are not committing yourself to an unrealistic schedule. These revisions are marked on the copy of your report attached to this message.

The use of the you viewpoint in this manner makes it feel as if the writer is taking an "us versus them" or "me versus you" approach to distance himself from a potential problem—as if to say "this is your problem, not mine." Instead, in the second Johnson and Gupta email message, the writer is formal, professional and polite without using *you*. The writer represents a department and is writing on its behalf to people who do not have to take the offered advice but who do need to hear it before making a decision. By not using *you*, the writer is actually more engaged in the situation.

Although there are problems with the report, the writer is positive: "The Johnson and Gupta proposal appears complete and thorough..." The writer transitions to the potential problem using the word *however*. However, the writer describes the *revisions* as *small* and the word *revisions* is not modified with words such as *urgent* or *required*. The writer also presents the benefit that will follow if the revisions are made: these revisions will "ensure that the company is not committing itself to an unrealistic schedule." Compare this way of expressing the thought versus the following:

"Making these revisions will ensure that you do not totally mess up the schedule."

I admit that I have exaggerated for effect, but do you see the difference? The *you* in the above line says the problem is all yours, not mine. In other words, although *you* can be inclusive, it can also feel like a command or an accusation or can distance the writer from the situation.

Ultimately, you have to decide if you will use the *you* viewpoint or not. And if you use it, you have to decide how often you will use it and the overall tone you want to establish, such as inclusionary or exclusionary, imperative or helpful.

What you want to do when you are engaged in business writing is to be aware of your choices and then make the choice that best helps you achieve your purpose. In short, it's up to you to choose the tone you will use and to ensure it is the right tone for the situation. More often than not, you will find that the use of a positive tone will help you produce the results you desire. That does not mean you should never use a negative tone; however, make sure the tone you use suits the topic, reader and situation.

Chapter 12: Promotional Email

As the name implies, promotional or sales email messages are used to promote or sell something to someone. In order to sell anyone anything, you have to persuade him or her to take action—to buy. However, if you are selling expensive (and possibly complex) products or services—IT solutions, backhoes for commercial construction use, accounting and auditing services—the action you desire might not be "buy" even though you are writing a sales or promotional email message. The reason? People don't purchase expensive and complex products off-the-shelf (or in response to a sales message) the way they buy DVDs, books or socks.

Instead, you might want the reader to take a pre-purchase action—call for more information, visit a website, arrange for a sales representative to call and so on. In short, before you write a sales or promotional email, or any copy meant to persuade for that matter, you need to know what action you are trying to persuade the reader to take. You would keep your ultimate goal, the sale, in mind but ask for the next step (the call, for instance) to be taken. If you don't know your purpose and the action you want the reader to take, how can you achieve your purpose and motivate the reader to take a specific action?

Knowing what you want the reader to do, and motivating the reader to do it, is at the heart of any persuasive message. However, anytime you want anyone to do something—even attend a meeting—you are "selling" and you have to motivate the person to act or respond (to buy into what you want, so to speak). For this chapter, though, we will concentrate on writing sales or promotional email messages.

The typical sales or promotional email does the following:

- Lets the reader know your purpose—why you are writing.
- Introduces you to the reader and makes a connection between you (your company, your products and/or services or your proposal) and the reader's problem, issue or opportunity.
- Demonstrates that you understand the client's objectives and, depending on the circumstance, how what you are selling or proposing relates to the client's objectives and/or target market.
- Extols the virtues of your company, products and/or services or summarizes and extols the virtues of your proposal.
- Calls for a defined action; motivates the reader to act.

Three-section sales or promotional email

Sales or promotional email should be divided into three sections:

Introduction

- Hooks reader (captures attention) with lines that relate to a problem, issue, opportunity or situation that the reader is familiar with or can relate to.
- Continues to hold the reader's interest by proposing a solution, alternative or means of exploiting the opportunity.
- Makes clear the purpose of the letter.

Body

- Continues to hold interest; influences attitude.
- May overcome anticipated objections (major attitude adjustment technique).
- May include rationale for and/or benefits of proposal.
- May include schedule (timelines) and a detailed projection of costs (proposed budget).
- May build trust in the writer (or the organization the writer represents).

Conclusion

- Calls for action and outlines next steps and how to take them; details who proposes to do what for whom, when, where and why.
- May offer an incentive to motivate the reader to act.
- Demonstrates willingness to answer questions or provide more details.

You might use attention-grabbing subheadings that create distinct sections in a sales letter but you do not have to. Either way, you should be aware that the role of each section is distinct. Even so, you need to write so that there are logical transitions between sections and a logical flow from section to section.

Spam or not?

Before we look more closely at sales or promotional email, let's address the elephant in the room. Isn't such email considered spam?

Email used for marketing purposes is not spam—as long as the recipient has given the mailer permission to send such email. Permission-based email eliminates the cost of printing brochures and the cost of mailing.

Long considered a lightweight in the advertising world and often confused with spam, email marketing has come a long way. However, it has a long way to go to reach the magnitude of traditional Direct Response Marketing (DRM). The billion dollars (and growing) spent on email marketing in 2012 may seem paltry in comparison with the $200-billion direct mail market, but email is gathering momentum while direct mail seems to have peaked.

The reason? Primarily cost. Email campaigns cost $5 to $7 per thousand, compared with the $500 to $750 (or more) per thousand for direct mail. Email promotions are quicker to execute, get faster results and their success (or failure) can be measured more easily (by click-throughs and sales the day the email lands).

Allow me to repeat this: Email marketing is not spam, if used on an opt-in or permission basis. However, there are risks to sending DRM email. Email users are so overwhelmed by spam these days that they use a number of filtering techniques to keep it out of their in-boxes. DRM email may be caught in spam filters. Occasionally, email users forget they granted permission for a marketer to send them email and they may view the DRM email as spam.

The challenge for email marketers is to make the message so relevant to the person receiving it that it is not confused with spam. In addition, the offer must be compelling enough to make the recipient act on it. With that in mind, email marketers should:

- Use strong, provocative or self-explanatory subject lines
- Keep the message to one computer screen (page)
- Include a link to a website for more information
- Include an incentive to click on the link
- Include unsubscribe information
- Ensure those who unsubscribe get off the list

Cold-call promotional email

Let's look at what we might describe as a cold-call sales or promotional email. Remember, though, the sender has to have permission to communicate with the reader. How to obtain permission goes beyond the scope of this book. Let's pretend that permission has been obtained. Here is the email:

Dear Ms. Bussman:

Are you having trouble keeping your cool? When you turn on the air conditioning, do you feel as if you are wasting energy and money? PLR Air Conditioning would like to demonstrate how we can help you keep cool and save energy too—all for less than you might have imagined.

We would like to demonstrate how the installation of a PLR air conditioning system will keep your plant and office cool and reduce energy costs. The demonstration takes 45 minutes, and will not disrupt your business operations.

We believe that you will find PLR systems to be practical, efficient and economical.

PLR has been in the industrial heating and air conditioning business for over 40 years, servicing companies like yours. We are a member of the Better Business Bureau and have a stellar credit rating. You can view our client list and read a number of testimonials on our website, www.plr.com.

Please review the information in the attached brochure and call us for a demonstration. What do you have to lose? Certainly not your cool! To set up a demonstration, call 416-555-5555.

If you call us by May 31, we will conduct a free energy efficiency audit and show you 10 no-cost ways to cut your company's electricity bill.

Sincerely,
James P. Callahan
Sales Manager

Components of cold-call promotional email

Now, let's examine the components of the sales email.

Introduction: The email starts with humor (risky, I confess) to capture the attention of (or hook) the reader. Notice how the word "cool" used in the introduction is related to the product. Notice also how quickly the writer connects the opening line to the product by connecting cool to air conditioning. By the third sentence, the reader knows exactly why the writer is writing (purpose)—to conduct a demonstration. Notice how the purpose is supported by a benefit statement implying cost savings. In other words, the writer is supporting his purpose by letting the reader know that PLR can solve a problem.

> Are you having trouble keeping your cool? When you turn on the air conditioning, do you feel as if you are wasting energy and money? PLR Air Conditioning would like to demonstrate how we can help keep you cool and save energy too—all for less than you might have imagined.

Body: Once the purpose is established, the body expands on it while maintaining interest and influencing attitude. The body overcomes a possible objection: *This will probably take all day*. No, it "takes 45 minutes." It also focuses on information that is of interest to the client by promising to "reduce the cost of energy" and to be "practical, efficient, economical."

We would like to demonstrate how the installation of a PLR air conditioning system will keep your plant and office cool and reduce the cost of energy. The demonstration takes 45 minutes, and it will not disrupt your business operations.

We believe that you will find PLR systems to be practical, efficient and economical.

The company also uses the body to build trust, just in case the reader is wondering who PLR is.

PLR has been in business for over 40 years, servicing companies like yours. We are a member of the Better Business Bureau and have a stellar credit rating. You can view our client list and read a number of testimonials on our website, www.plr.com.

Conclusion: Here the email asks the reader to do something—read an attached brochure and call. The conclusion succinctly summarizes what the email has been about and echoes the opening, as if reminding the reader what caught her attention in the first place—"What do you have to lose? Certainly not your cool!"

The conclusion also offers the reader a limited time incentive to act. Within ten days, PLR will know how effective its cold-call sales email was. If the company sends out five hundred email messages and has twenty or so replies, the letter would be considered a success. With that in mind, if you are ever conducting a direct mail campaign, sample your audience first. Say you want to send out two thousand emails. Send out a hundred first and gauge the response. If you come up empty, you will want to review and revise your sales message.

Follow-up sales message

In the post-demonstration follow-up sales email, the same principles apply. The writer does not have to work as hard at hooking the reader but the writer must still capture the reader's attention. Analyze the letter to see how the structure adheres to the introduction, body, conclusion methodology of writing persuasive cold-call sales letters.

Dear Ms. Bussman:

We hope you were able to see how a PLR air conditioning system would provide energy efficiency, cool comfort and the maximum return on your investment when we demonstrated the system for you on October 30.

We would like to thank Mr. Lindsay and Mrs. Smooth from your operations division for joining us for the demonstration.

As discussed, the equipment PLR proposes to install is modular in design, so you can add additional units as the need arises. This makes it practical, efficient and economical, both now and in the future. Therefore, the system protects you against obsolescence as your business continues to grow.

I will follow up on the attached proposal on November 11. The information it provides should answer any pricing and timing questions you might have. However, if you require additional information before November 11, please call me.

In addition, I have attached the results of your free energy efficiency audit showing you 10 no-cost ways to cut your energy bill.

Sincerely,
James P. Callahan
Sales Manager

Promotional email exercise

See if you can put the sales letter writing principles into effect by writing a sales or promotional email message. Think of something you might have to sell or would like to sell and compose your message following the three-section promotional email approach.

Before you start, ask yourself the W5 questions. In particular, ask the following questions: What am I writing about? What's my purpose? What is in it for the reader? What objections do I anticipate? How should I overcome them? Do I have to build trust? What is the action that I am trying to motivate? When am I trying to motivate it? How or where does the reader take it? What incentive can I offer to motivate action?

Your letter should build from capturing attention to asking for the action you want to take place. In between, you want to hold interest and influence attitude. Otherwise, action will not be taken.

So go forth and write in a promotional manner.

Take some time to outline and write a sales or promotional email before you read on.

Appendix One

Sample than-you note

Here is a sample thank-you note, with subject line, that was written following the W5 outline process:

> **Subject**: Thank you for the opportunity
>
> I wish to thank you for the confidence you have shown in me by promoting me to dispatch. I am excited about the challenges this position offers and look forward to learning as fast as I can so that I can contribute to the success of the company.
>
> Your confidence in me is appreciated. I will work hard to meet your expectations, as this is a great opportunity.
>
> Sincerely,
> Janice Lake

Notice that the subject line conveys a clear sense of purpose. It does not just say "thank you" but it includes "the opportunity." The why, or the reason the writer is writing, is there—*thank you*—as is what the writer is thanking the reader for—*the opportunity*. When you write, look at your W5 and try to convey the most important elements in your subject line.

Just as the body of a report elaborates on a report's executive summary, the opening of an email message elaborates on the most important elements of the subject line. In this case, we see more of the why and what in the opening line. Notice that the rest of the opening paragraph supports that opening line. This is called focus. In other words, the message does not digress into other topics. Also, notice that the closing paragraph acts as a summary of the message.

This repetition, restatement and elaboration (without becoming redundant) is required to achieve focus and to ensure the reader gets your message. You will see this method used in effective email messages, letters, proposals and reports.

In this particular message, there is no call to action and no request for feedback, nor does the message require one.

If you are saying you could have written the thank-you note without asking the W5 questions, I will not argue with you. However, you would have written a different message—similar, perhaps, but different. The more complex a message is, the more important it is to ask the W5 questions before you write. In short, develop a W5 habit no matter what you want to write and you will be more likely to include all the information your reader needs.

Sample email messages

Below are several sample email messages. See if you can find the who, what, where, when, why and/or how. Not all elements will be found in every message. Part of your job, as mentioned, is to determine what to put in and what to leave out of anything you write. Also, ask yourself the following:

- Is the "why" or purpose of the email message clear and up front?
- Are the benefits and/or consequences (or anything else that might influence attitude) detailed?
- Is the required or desired action—if action is required or desired—clearly expressed?

Note: Avoid anger, sarcasm or extreme emotion in business writing. However, when writing a consumer-to-business (or consumer-to-politician) message, you might get away with a modest amount of emotion or humor. For instance, I like the humorous subject line of the first email below, but notice how the humor is related to the subject matter and how the message starts with a clear purpose.

Subject: Take this snow and shovel it!

Dear Municipal Councilor Johnson,

I'm writing to resolve the issue about snow removal after a snowfall.

During the recent heavy snowfall, a few of my neighbors shoveled snow from their driveways and dumped it on city property. Unfortunately, they piled their snow at the front and back of other people's vehicles, making it difficult to exit the parking spaces. This became a point of frustration for many of the car owners.

Would your office be able to send out notices to the residents of my neighborhood to remind them that there is a snow removal bylaw they must adhere to? If you could provide me with a response by the end of the week, it would be greatly appreciated.

Sincerely,
Sidney Smith

◾ ◾ ◾

Subject: Sorry for missing lunch

Dear Janine,

After speaking to your husband, I realize that my absence from a recent networking lunch that I had agreed to attend upset you and I would like to apologize for missing the gathering.

There were several last-minute scheduling changes at work but I should have called you. I am sorry for not doing so.

Your friendship means a great deal to me. I look forward to seeing you at lunch next month.

Sincerely,
Terri

◼ ◼ ◼

Subject: Sincerest appreciation for your help

Dear Laura,

It has been a week since I started my new job and I could not have landed the promotion without your help. I just wanted to thank you for your support. Because of your assistance, I was able to produce significant results and impress our supervisor who gave me the recommendation that opened the door to the job interview.

I would like to invite you for dinner this weekend and thank you personally. Please let me know over the next day or two if you are available. You can email or call me.

Best regards,
Sally

◼ ◼ ◼

Subject: Apology for missing the lab meeting

Dear Dr. Jones,

I apologize for missing the lab meeting this morning and for the inconvenience I may have caused. Unfortunately, the subway I was on got stuck at Bloor and Yonge and was out of service for 40 minutes.

I was supposed to share the results of my work with my colleagues. I will email my results later today to you and to my lab partners so that they have the most up-to-date information on my project.

If you have any questions about my results, please email me or talk to me at the next lab meeting.

Sincerely,
Sally

◼ ◼ ◼

Subject: Written Warning

It has become necessary to again remind you of your responsibilities. Since issuing a verbal warning two weeks ago, we have not seen improvements in the following areas:

- arriving at work at the scheduled time
- matching your paperwork to the product being loaded
- giving appropriate notice of non-work-related appointments

Immediate improvements in these areas are expected. They are necessary to ensure customer satisfaction. Your work-related performance will be reviewed daily.

Failure to comply with this request immediately will lead to further disciplinary action up to, and including, termination. If you have any questions, email me.

Sincerely,
Jane Lake

◼ ◼ ◼

Subject: Overdue payment reminder

Dear Ms. Lam,

Our records indicate that payment of your account in the amount of $6,890 is 30 days overdue. A copy of invoice #181 is attached.

If the payment has been forwarded, please disregard this email. Otherwise, please submit payment by October 23.

If you are unable to submit your payment, please email or call (416) 555-1212 so that we can discuss and resolve the issue. Thank you for your cooperation.

Sincerely,
Sally Arnold

◼ ◼ ◼

Subject: Tiffany sofa payment

Dear Ms. Williams,

Furniture Gallery is confident that you are enjoying the Tiffany sofa that you purchased last March at the Main Street location. You took advantage of our "no money down for six months" special and we are now at the end of the sixth month. To ensure that you can continue to enjoy the sofa, we need to receive your first payment by March 14.

You can make your payment by cash, check or credit card (Visa or MasterCard) at the Main Street location. If you have any questions, please reply to this email or call (416) 555-1212.

Sincerely,
Gail Jones

■ ■ ■

The apology email below is particularly effective. The writer explains what happened, takes full responsibility, offers the reader appropriate compensation and assures the reader it will not happen again—in three focused, concise paragraphs.

Subject: Apologies for missing Saturday's lesson

Dear Mr. Tanaka,

I would like to apologize for my scheduling mistake. During our last meeting, we decided to conduct our next training session on Saturday. I did not have my day planner with me so I could not record the date. Because we usually meet Sundays, the date slipped my mind. This does not excuse what happened and I assure you that it will not happen again.

Your time is valuable, so to compensate you for the lost time and the inconvenience there will be no charge for the next lesson.

I apologize again for my scheduling mistake and look forward to seeing you on Sunday, March 14, at 1 pm.

Regards,
George Thompson

Appendix One

Appendix Two

Hotel case study sample leads

I want to stress one last time the importance of defining your true business purpose before you write. The purpose, as you define it, directly influences the words you write, the tone you use and any action you request.

For instance, in the hotel case study, you had to write an opening paragraph to the manager of the Chelsea Hotel in London, Ontario. You had a negative experience at the hotel; however, you use the hotel on a regular basis because it's conveniently located and offers reasonable rates. So what is your purpose? Do you want a full or partial refund? Or do you want assurance that the problems will be fixed before you book your next business trip?

If you are angry and want a full refund, here's what you might write:

> I stayed at your hotel last week and was extremely unhappy with the service. The food was cold, the room was a mess and some of your staff members were rude. I am not at all satisfied and would like a full refund ASAP.

I am *not* suggesting the above passage is solidly written, but it does convey a particular purpose. However, if you said that your purpose was to obtain a refund, I'd suggest you might want to think again. From the case study: "You travel to London every quarter on business. Your company has used this hotel for several years because it is conveniently located and... offers reasonable rates."

With that in mind, how would you feel if you obtained a refund and the service did not improve the next time you were there? What would you have achieved? So I repeat: determine your *true* business purpose before you write.

If you want assurance that the problems will be fixed before you book your next business trip, this is what you might write:

> Last week I stayed at your hotel and encountered several service-related issues. Due to business in London, I had planned to stay at your hotel four times a year. However, I need your assurance that service levels will improve before I commit to doing so.

In workshops, people have asked me if they can ask for assurance that conditions will improve *and* a refund. What happens if the manager grants you a refund but conditions are just as poor the next time you are there? What happens if the manager does not give you a refund? What is your primary purpose? Do you want to find a new, more expensive, less conveniently located hotel?

The fact is, by asking for two things—a refund and improved conditions—you muddy the water. Instead of assuring you that conditions were improved, the manager might fight your request for a refund. That may be a sign of a poor manager but that is not your issue—not if your primary business purpose is to be assured that conditions at the hotel have improved.

In short, you want to determine your true business purpose and focus on that. For instance, if you were a consumer who had stayed at the hotel in a resort area during a vacation and had experienced poor service and poor conditions, I could understand if you asked for a refund. That purpose makes sense.

For the sake of argument, let's say you disagree with the purpose I am suggesting. In other words, you might decide that your business purpose is to obtain a refund. You will write a different email, based on your purpose, than I will write based on my purpose. That is the point of this exercise: to understand that purpose influences the words you use, the tone you use and the action you request.

◼ ◼ ◼

Furniture case study sample lead

Here is a possible lead for the furniture case study letter:

> I hope you can resolve a problem with my furniture order. On November 1, I ordered office furniture from the Office Company catalogue but two chairs were missing when my order arrived. I called to sort this out and, on November 11, I received one additional chair; however, it was the wrong color. The person I talked to about my order no longer works for you and no one seems to know about my problem. I would like you to sort this out for me by the end of the week.

I have chosen to open this letter with my purpose—to get help solving the problem. Then I give some background information (because the recipient is not familiar with my problem), reiterate my purpose and include a deadline.

Even though I have included a deadline, I do not spell out any consequences, such as: "I would like you to sort this out for me by the end of the week or I will return all the furniture that I have purchased at your store." If the manager does not call and assure me the problem will be sorted out, I can escalate my complaint and include consequences.

Of course the letter would continue beyond the first paragraph to include additional background information, such as the invoice number and model numbers of the chairs that did not arrive. I would end by reiterating my call to action and include my phone number and email address.

By providing a deadline—the end of the week—I know that I can follow up by a specific time and escalate the complaint (if the issue has not been resolved).

There are other ways to word the opening paragraph but what I want to reiterate is this: if you want to capture the attention of your reader off the top, include your purpose in your opening paragraph.

If you wanted to include a shorter deadline in your letter—say you needed the furniture sooner for a particular business reason—you can do that. The point is, before you write, you have to think about what you need, why you need it and when you need it. That way you can write a clear, concise, coherent, focused message that starts with your purpose, establishes an appropriate tone, includes relevant background information, adjusts the attitude of the reader and includes a clear and appropriate call to action.

◼ ◼ ◼

Sample email from Trinket to Widget

Below I've set up the sample email from Trinket to Widget. Notice how the purpose is alluded to in the subject line and clearly stated in the opening paragraph. The body of the email provides background information required to support the purpose but does not rehash old issues that have been resolved. The tone is positive and the concluding paragraph states who will do what next and when. The action reinforces the writer's purpose. Note: the writer and reader have done business together before, so the salutation is not as formal as a letter might be.

◼ ◼ ◼

Subject: Resolving problem with shipment of widgets

Hi Tom,

We require your assistance in resolving a recent shipment problem. Our last order of widgets from Widget Inc. was short shipped and had a higher than normal fault rate and we need your assurance this will not occur again.

The shortage came at a busy time for Trinket Ltd. and we were unable to fill all our orders. Although we had surplus widgets, we did not have enough to compensate for the short shipment and the increased fault rate.

Floor-Mart, our largest customer, was upset by the shortage of Trinkets and has threatened to take its business elsewhere. If that happens, both our companies will lose significant business. In an effort to ensure that this problem does not occur again, we must receive your assurance that:

- future orders will be shipped in full
- quality control issues will be addressed

Trinket Ltd. and Widget Inc. have had a strong business relationship over the last year, one that we hope to continue.

Once we have your assurance about future shipments, we would like to arrange a meeting to discuss the outstanding accounting issues, which I am confident we can resolve so that we can continue our mutually profitable relationship. I will follow up with a phone call to set up the meeting. In the meantime, if you have any questions, please contact me.

Sincerely,
Sharon Selma
Chief Executive Officer

◼ ◼ ◼

Sample email from Widget to Trinket

The purpose in the email below is clear: to assure Trinket that the issue has been resolved. Notice, however, how the email starts with an apology and that there is no attempt by Widget to blame the third-party maintenance company. There is also an effort to sort out the invoice issue. It won't go away by itself, so it must be addressed. The concluding paragraph restates the apology and invites Trinket to call if there are any questions.

Subject: Resolving under-shipment of widgets

Hi Sharon,

Please accept my apologies for the under-shipment of widgets, and the higher than normal fault rate, in your last order. Quality is important to Widget and I want to assure you that we have identified and fixed our recent manufacturing problem. We can now guarantee that we will be shipping full orders with acceptable fault levels.

I also want you to know that we will now maintain a surplus inventory of widgets. Should a problem occur, we will be able to ship your full order. Should you require a rush order of additional widgets, we will be able to accommodate you.

Once again, I would like to apologize for the shipment issue and hope to continue supplying high-quality widgets to Trinket.

We will adjust your invoice to reflect the short shipment and will deduct the cost of all faulty widgets. Please contact me by the end of the week if you have any questions concerning this.

Sincerely,
Tom Kohl
CEO
Widget Inc.

Appendix Three

Passive voice converted to active voice

The passive sentences presented in Chapter 9 have been converted to the active voice below.

More than one third of the applicants to the school failed the entrance exam.

She slammed on the brakes as the car sped downhill.

I have damaged your bicycle.

The thief damaged your bicycle.

The committee is considering action on the bill.

By then, the sound engineers will have completely remixed the soundtrack.

I wrote the paper on a computer to satisfy the instructor's demands for legibility.

The student wrote the paper on a computer to satisfy the instructor's demands for legibility.

Appendix Four

"Wall of words" suggested revision

Canadian furniture manufacturers want to sell products to the growing U.S. healthcare furniture market but they lag far behind their U.S. counterparts. However, there are ways they can achieve this goal.

Driven by an aging population and the need to replace obsolete facilities, ABC Research Co. estimates that the value of the U.S. market for healthcare furniture will grow by 50%, reaching approximately $1.7 billion by 2012. Growth will occur primarily in the clinical segment of this market.

Regional office furniture and clinical furniture manufacturers currently supply the majority of the healthcare furniture market, but national American furniture manufacturers have made significant investments in clinical products.

To gain entry into this market, Canadian furniture manufacturers should acquire small U.S. suppliers specializing in healthcare furniture.

About the Author

Based in Toronto, Ontario, Canada, Paul Lima has been a professional writer and writing instructor for over 25 years. He has run a successful freelance writing and business-writing training business since 1988.

For corporate clients, Paul writes media releases, promotional content, case studies, sales letters, direct-response brochures, website copy and other material

For newspapers and magazines, Paul writes about small business and technology issues. His articles have appeared in the *Globe and Mail, Toronto Star, National Post, Backbone, Profit*, CBC.ca and many other publications.

As a qualified educator, Paul conducts seminars on business-writing, media interview preparation and freelance writing.

An English major from York University, Paul has worked as an advertising copywriter, continuing education manager and magazine editor.

Paul is the author of several books, listed below. Read more about him online at www.paullima.com.

Books by Paul Lima:

- *Harness the Email Writing Process: How to Become a More Effective and Efficient Email Writer*
- *Harness the Business Writing Process: Email, Letters, Proposals, Reports, Media Releases, Web Content*
- *How to Write Web Copy and Social Media Content*
- *Copywriting That Works: Bright ideas to Help You Inform, Persuade, Motivate and Sell!*
- *Fundamentals of Writing: How to Write Articles, Media Releases, Case Studies, Blog Posts and Social Media Content*
- *How To Write A Non-Fiction Book in 60 Days*
- *Produce, Price and Promote Your Self-Published Fiction or Non-fiction Book and eBook*
- *Everything You Wanted to Know About Freelance Writing: Find, Price, Manage Corporate Writing Assignments & Develop Article Ideas and Sell Them to Newspapers and Magazines*
- *Unblock Writer's Block: How to Face It, Deal with It and Overcome It*
- *(re)Discover the Joy of Creative Writing*

- *How to Write Media Releases to Promote Your Business, Organization or Event*
- *Are You Ready For Your Interview? How to Prepare for Media Interviews. Prepare for interviews with print and broadcast reporters.*
- *Rebel in the Back Seat and other short stories*

Available online through www.paullima.com/books

www.ingramcontent.com/pod-product-compliance
Lightning Source LLC
Chambersburg PA
CBHW051226200326
41519CB00025B/7270